Overcoming

David Wingate

ISBN: 979-8-89397-525-3
Edition: First
Published by Elite Scribes Book Writing

Table of Contents

The Back Story

Before I tell you my story, I would like to share my purpose and inspiration for writing this book. First of all, it has been a burden on my heart to do this for some time now, but life has been busy, and there has never seemed to be time to do it. This winter, 2024/2025 seems to have slowed somewhat. I now understand why I had to wait. You see, the subject matter of this book was not yet completed in my life enough to write it, and it will never be fully complete until the long years of my life are over. God calls me home. Now seems to be a time when my understanding of the subject has become mature enough and time to write on it has presented itself so I am going to do the best I can while I can.

In life, we all have things that we aspire to be or things that we would like to accomplish—a bucket list, if you will. Everyone's bucket list is different, depending on life experiences, things we like or dislike, and how we are generally built as a person. I know that many Christians have heard the term "overcomer" or some term containing the same meaning. However, I am not sure that many understand what being an overcomer means.

What does it mean to be called an overcomer? Or what does the Bible mean when it says, "and they overcame Him by the Blood of the Lamb and Word of their testimony." Much of the Bible is no more than a recorded piece of a person's life during a time when they had obstacles to overcome and how they overcame those obstacles, rather than how they relied on God to overcome them in their lives. While we know the Bible to be a story about one man's life and His lineage here on this earth, that is to say, Jesus Christ and all of those who carried that bloodline from Adam and Eve to Mary who conceived of the Holy Spirit, to bare the Son of God; we also know it is a series of lessons on how one ought to live by faith in God. Knowing this, we are none of us perfect in ourselves, nor indeed can we be, but it is God who works in us to overcome this world. In this fashion and by the grace of God, our Father, I will endeavor to share my own life experiences and how God intervened to make me an overcomer.

I don't say that to mean that I have, in fact, completed this task of overcoming, nor do I have a prescription to do so other than to point you to the ONE that has overcome both this world and the evil one, who seeks to devour all that was created in the endeavor to be able to declare himself to be the Most High.

Having said this, I ask that you read this account of my life with the understanding that I am still a work in progress and I have much more to learn as God has not yet seen it as a fit time to call me home. I pray that when He does, I may hear Him say, "Well done, my good and faithful servant, enter into my rest," wherewith He has redeemed us by the blood of His own son. Throughout this account, you will see many points which God has called me to overcome. And He has repeatedly delivered me from this world, the evil one, and at times myself, so that He may make me His own. I give glory to Him always, and I hope that this may be an encouraging word to you to face the trials you, too, have and will encounter. God bless, and be encouraged today.

To overcome is not merely to survive adversity but to grow spiritually and emotionally through it. This book is both a personal testimony and a spiritual roadmap, reflecting on moments when God's grace, forgiveness, and purpose were most evident in my life.

Scriptures that Guide this Journey:

- **Revelation 12:11** – "They overcame him by the blood of the Lamb and by the word of their testimony."

- **Jeremiah 29:11** – "'For I know the plans I have for you,' declares the Lord..."

- **Psalm 37** – Encouragement to trust in the Lord and do good.

I was born in 1971, the youngest of ten children, in a home built by my father with little formal education but abundant faith. From a young age, I was immersed in church and came to know Jesus at age seven, baptized at eight, and baptized in the Holy Spirit by thirteen.

Psalm 37 – "Delight yourself in the Lord, and He will give you the desires of your heart."

We lived in a house my dad built on property that was given to him by his father. I don't remember a whole lot about Wingate Dr., as we moved away when I was very young. My parents were struggling financially, but for the most part, we kids never really felt it that much. Somehow, there were always Christmas presents and a few new clothes for school. We never went hungry, and there was plenty of love to fill in for whatever material things we might have lacked. I came to know Jesus at about age seven and was baptized when I was 8 years old. I never really understood how significant that was until I became quite a bit older. I grew up in church, hearing the Word of the Lord and always singing His praises. There were hard times, just like in any family, but Mom and Dad somehow managed to always look on the brighter side of things. Growing up in this way set a foundation for me that, in my youth, I took for granted. At about 12 or 13, I remember receiving the Holy Spirit's baptism and feeling God's power in me like never before.

We attended church a lot and were involved in many different ministries. Boys Brigade and Pioneer Girls, youth group, and music, to name a few. My parents always picked up additional people to bring them to church to hear what God was doing and what He had done for them.

I still remember the noon whistle that would blow from the Temperance Fire Department when we were eating lunch. And the preschool lessons mom taught us on the back porch of the house. I remember learning to ride a bike up and down Wingate Dr. and playing with the neighbor girl. We had some animals there, such as rabbits, chickens, and goats. And we had a swimming pool. For a man without a high school diploma, my dad did quite well taking care of a family of 12, and now, when I look back, I can't imagine how they did it, Mom and he.

In Winter 1987, ten years have passed since my parents bought the farm; no, they didn't die; they actually bought a farm. In 1977, my parents moved from Wingate Dr. out to Ida, where they had purchased 10 acres in hopes of giving their 10 children a better place to live. It was not that Wingate Dr was the problem; it was the school system, rather the things that the school was allowing us to be exposed to that they did not like. Sometimes, the best way to overcome a problem is to avoid it.

The year we moved to the farm, there was a blizzard, and it was a hard winter, though my memories of it are few and rather blurry at best. You see, I was only 7 years old at the time, and there were many changes occurring that year: new house, new school, new friends. I remember this winter, the winter of 87, well, however. Life at this point was at a zenith. I was 17 now and knew enough to feel like I was about ready to make my own life adventure. We were involved in church school and 4-H activities; my mom loved every bit of it. My dad had built the farmhouse we lived in, and we were eating food that we had grown ourselves on the farm; this was mom's dream. Regular church attendance and involvement were staples in our lives, and all was well.

We were up North that winter visiting members of an associated church, and their boy and I were out on a long winter day enjoying some sledding on the hills. It was cold, but the fun we were having kept us out all day. The next day, I didn't feel well, and by the time we were headed home back to Ida, which was a 5-hour trip, I was a complete wreck. What followed would perhaps be the first real trial of my faith and would last for many years. Maybe this is because this trial would become the teacher of many life lessons necessary to becoming an overcomer. Whatever the purpose was, it has yielded fruit in me that may not have come otherwise.

After the trip home from sledding, I went to the hospital, where I stayed for the next couple of weeks with a horrible kidney infection. The next several years would become a series of hospital stays, a lot of missed school time, and many, many days of just not feeling well at all. There were a couple of surgeries and a lot of time spent recovering from them. I missed almost the whole last marking period of my junior year of high school, for which I had to spend time after school for most of my senior year, making it up so that I could graduate with my class. Even after graduation, there would be more doctor visits and procedures to get everything functioning properly for the next several years. The final end of it would not come until some other trials had come. During the worst part of the kidney trial, I felt that my dad really wasn't very empathetic or compassionate for me. It seemed he viewed me as weak, and at times, it was even painfully evident that this was the case. This would cause a tremendous amount of pain for me and a feeling that I was never good enough. For many years, I carried hurt and resentment over this, and it wasn't till many years later, when he became ill, that he would apologize for this. Forgiveness was hard for me to find, and there was some resentment that caused a strained relationship with Dad for the rest of his life. I have forgiven him, and now that my kids are grown, I can say that I understand to a point why he felt the way he did.

This season, spanning from 1987 to 1997, marked my first prolonged trial. It wasn't just about physical healing—it was also a spiritual crucible, pressing me toward deeper faith and reflection.

Forgiveness is essential to becoming an overcomer, for we cannot have victory while harboring unforgiveness. Something else I was learning throughout this time was that Jesus is with us and feels our pain. He cries with us and laughs with us, but He is always there. He does not condemn us for our shortcomings; rather, He teaches us how to do better and gives us victory in areas where we struggle.

Matthew 6:14–15 – Forgiveness is not optional; it opens the door for healing.

To make matters worse, my choice of spouse did not help the strained relationship between my dad and me. I was a shy and somewhat withdrawn young man who had a very hard time talking with other kids, especially girls. The kidney issues only exacerbated this, and so I found myself just kind of rolling along, waiting for a girl to talk to me. My first experience with a serious relationship was with a girl who was in the church and was approved of and encouraged by my parents.

I dated April for about 6 months before she broke it off. I was devastated and had no desire to get back into a relationship. I was working at McDonalds at the time, and Kris was working there as well. She had seen something she liked in me and asked me out on a date. Then she asked me again. The third time she asked, I said I would go. She was 6 years older than me; at 18, that's a big deal. My dad didn't like it one bit. He sought to break it up however he could. Kris didn't back away, and this just made me more convinced that she was the one for me. I loved her because she loved me first. This relationship, however, would drive a deepening wedge between my dad and I. Kris had been married before, and there was a lingering relationship with her ex-husband that was confusing to me, but it did not seem to hinder our relationship. She would continue to withdraw from that relationship as ours grew, but it was a strain for a time. Things got bad between Dad and me, and after a fight over a late night out, I decided to move out.

At first, I didn't want to live with Kris, so I lived in my car and stayed at a friend's house from time to time. Eventually, I moved in with Kris, but I was never at peace about living with her after we had left marriage. One morning, we were getting ready for work, and she announced to me she was pregnant. I wanted to fix this right away. I was ready to get married, but she wasn't. So, I lied to everyone and told them we eloped to get the pressure off of me about living with a woman outside of marriage. Kris returned the favor and made me ask for her hand 5 times before she said yes. Eventually, she married me on the day after Tyler, our first son, was born. The marriage was supposed to fix all the wrongs. My father had to accept her now as my wife; we were no longer living in sin, and I wouldn't be a "weekend dad." While this "fixed" all that was wrong, it did not completely heal either of my relationships.

Forgiveness was needed to overcome. All through this time, God remained close to me, and I often spent many hours in prayer over the things that were troubling me. Prayer is a powerful and necessary tool for living an overcomer's life. We need the strength that we receive through prayer, and we need God to intervene when we are not able.

I was carrying a lot during that time — a relationship with Kris, a job, college, and living in my car while also dealing with a strained relationship with my dad and recurring kidney issues. I had started pre-med right out of high school and was doing well academically. However, the strain of everything became overwhelming, and something had to give. I became ill again and took an Incomplete for the semester, hoping that things would somehow settle down so I could continue. They didn't. Ultimately, I had to drop out of college. Still, I remained drawn to the medical field, so I enrolled in an EMT course and became a certified and licensed EMT. I had just finished before Tyler was born and applied to some jobs that paid next to nothing. So, I stayed at McDonald's and was able to get a second job at Walmart, which was just opening in Monroe.

I had been in a car accident that totaled my car, so I was walking and riding buses and sharing the car with Kris, who was also working two jobs now. Thank God for her job at Monroe Medical because it provided the insurance for Tyler to be born. We were determined to make this all work and somehow get the train back on the tracks. One night, somewhere in the midst of all of this, we were at my parent's house, and somehow, some way, in the middle of strained relationships and overworked and stressed out, Dad sat down with Kris and me at the table and shared with Kris why she needed Jesus. The Holy Spirit found His way into the conversation, and Kris accepted Jesus as Lord and Savior. Praise God because that's the only way any of this works. We quickly made some plans to get married before the birth, but Tyler came early, and we were married the day after he was born, April 3rd and 4th, 1992.

Kris and I had overcome many odds, obstacles, and blockades and had begun a family. A family which believed in Jesus and sought to keep Him at the center of everything. Of course, more trials would come, as well as more opportunities to exercise forgiveness, but we were together, and Jesus said that He would build His church upon the rock of His salvation, and the gates of Hell would not prevail against it. The family unit is the simplest of churches, with the man at the head to be the protector of his family and the woman supporting him to keep him strong in the face of trials. This is God's prescription, and when we follow God's way of doing things, this is another way we will become overcomers.

That first year together was great. We were in love and had overcome so much, both together and individually. We were living upstairs in an old farmhouse that the owner, Rose, had converted into an apartment while she lived downstairs. Life was very simple: work and home. Rent, daycare, and utilities made up the bulk of the bills, but when you make $25K to $30K a year from 4 jobs, there is not a lot to go around. We were happy, though, just keeping to ourselves for the most part, trying to figure things out.

That year, in the fall, we had another tragedy strike. Rose's daughter-in-law lived next door, and she had two boys she was raising alone because their dad had passed away. The boys were always in trouble, and they were trying to support bad habits by theft. One day, we came home from work and found our apartment had been broken into, and some of our things had been stolen. We knew who had done it but had no solid proof. Fearing that this would happen again, we decided we needed to find a new place to live. We didn't have the money to put down for a security deposit and the first month's rent, so Kris went to her employer, and they forwarded her the pay to do it. We moved into a small apartment complex in

Monroe, which was in many ways better than where we were. It was late fall when we moved, and the air was getting cooler. The new apartment was closer to Kris's job and daycare, which was good for working around the one-car issue. We would start our mornings by all of us piling into the car to get Tyler off to daycare, drop me off at work, and finally, Kris getting to work herself. I would ride the bus from Walmart to McDonalds, then from McDonalds to the downtown bus depot, and walk from there to the medical office where Kris worked to get the car. Then I would go pick up Tyler and then Kris and head back home at the end of a long day. By this time, Kris was making enough money at the medical office to leave McDonalds, so we were now working three jobs and had more income!

Romans 8:28 – "All things work together for good for those who love God."

After the winter of 1992-1993, Kris and I celebrated our first anniversary with a long weekend at home and a break from work. And wouldn't you know it, she conceived again! As crazy as it sounds, we were so excited. This time, there was less worry, incomes had continued to rise, and insurance was good. I was finally able to get a second car and started working on a career path with Walmart. I moved into the automotive department there and became the shop manager, and the pay was getting better. I had been working to get another car and ended up finding one that needed a lot of work. It was a good opportunity to learn more about auto mechanics and get some cheap transportation. I still worked the second job, but it was a lot easier with two cars now and more money. When we had time that summer, we would go for walks downtown and enjoy some fresh air and sunshine. We often took Tyler to the park and just sat and watched the river. We did not attend church often; we simply did not have the time, and I often worked on Sundays. When we did attend, we went to church where my dad was an elder, and I would play my guitar for the music program. Kris was a young, growing Christian, and we both had a lot to learn about marriage and priorities, especially myself.

As we became more financially stable, we worked and church attendance increased. I was leading music at times, and everything seemed to be going well. The pastor had asked me several times if we could move closer to the church. Looking back now, I know that was a very selfish thing to ask, and he gave little to no consideration for our situations or feelings in the matter. We were dealing with a lot of constant changes in life, and stability in anything was like gold. Kris and another woman were let go from the medical office for no reason. They were both expecting at the time, and the office brought on two replacements, one of which was an older man beyond the child-rearing years and the other a woman who could no longer have children either. A lawsuit was filed, and a small settlement was awarded. It was very small. The settlement was about the equivalent of six months' salary, and Kris had to find a new job when the baby came. She was able to get in at Target, which was opening soon in Monroe. Aaron was born on New Year's Eve 1993, and we had to make more adjustments with a new baby. I was full of zeal for the Lord and wanted to do the right things, but I began to add pressure to an already fairly high-stress situation. At the insistence of the pastor, I told Kris we were moving to Toledo, but she did not want to go.

It meant moving away from her hometown, her job, and my job and figuring out where the boys would go while we both worked. It was not a good thing to do. I ended up pressuring Kris into moving down to Toledo anyway so that we could be "closer to the church" where the pastor could "minister to us better." That would lead to the worst year of our marriage and nearly cost us the marriage entirely.

Were it not for many, many hours of prayer and seeking to understand God's Word, we would not have made it.

Sometimes, men will use their position to gain power, even in the church, perhaps even more so in the church, where people are the most vulnerable. This was definitely the case here. But God is present with us even in this.

Even when men have abused their position in the body of Christ and have set themselves above others to glorify themselves and not God.

Be Careful Who You Follow

1994 was a horrific year for Kris and I. I moved from Walmart to Sam's Club in Toledo and started a job at the local McDonalds. Kris was transferred to the Toledo store after working at Target for just a short time. Looking back, I don't know why she stayed with me at all. I clearly did not have her interest at heart. I thought of myself and my position. In a good marriage, the other person comes before ourselves. Ephesians 5 is one of the best pictures of this. When it says:

Ephesians 5 – "Husbands, love your wives as Christ loved the church."

We were fighting a lot because of the move, and neither the pastor nor the church was of any help. In fact, they only made things worse. Kris stopped attending, and at one point, Pastor Gary told me that there was a "spirit of divorce in our marriage," at which point I also stopped attending. I was devastated, and Kris decided that things had gotten so bad that she was going to look for a way out. She began a relationship with a co-worker and became unfaithful in the marriage. But if we look at what unfaithfulness really is, I was the one who was unfaithful to her by putting the church before my wife.

18

One night, she wrecked my car after being out late with her friends. At that point, I knew she was having an affair, but I had no solid proof. She kept telling me she was leaving, and I had enough, so I told her to go. I even changed the locks on the apartment door. Things were as bad as they get. Soon after that night, God got a hold of me and said why are you doing this? I never said you should put the church before your family. I made the decision then and there that I was moving back to Monroe, no matter the cost.

While all this was happening, I got a new job at Western Auto as a mechanic and tested and received several ASE certifications. My pay was increasing, as was Kris's; she was promoted to team leader at Target. So, at the end of the one-year lease, we were able to afford a house in Monroe, and we moved back to Monroe, bruised and battered by the church. While we were in Toledo, we bought a used Chevy Safari van and a used S10 pickup. I look back at the growth that God continued to bring despite the trials and lessons being learned, and I see His constant blessing and interventions throughout my life.

Psalms 37 – "Commit thyself unto the Lord in all thy ways, and He shall establish you in the land where you dwell."

There was still a lot of healing that needed to take place in our marriage, and there would be many times I would reflect back on this hard lesson learned, but 1995 would be a turning toward a stronger marriage that could weather storms and keep Christ at the centre.

At the time we were moving into the house and back to Monroe, Kris's sister had fallen on some hard times in her life and needed a place to go. The house was bigger than we needed, so after some arranging with the landlord, she moved in with us. Sometimes in life, we seem to go from one bad thing to another as if we cannot see which way is up. Having her sister move in with us was not ideal, but adding another trial at a time when we were already under strain strangely seemed to strengthen our resolve to bring this marriage back together.

On top of that, we had helped her mother move to Florida, and things didn't work out for her down there, so they wanted to move back and had no place to go. So, her mom and brother moved into the basement. Talk about a stressful situation. Her sister had a son, and we had two boys. Her mom and her brother are now all living under one roof on the heels of a very bad year Kris and I went through. To top it all off,

Kris and I were paying all the bills. What could go wrong? Not what you think, that's what. Her sister exercised no discipline in her son's life and would not allow anyone else to do so either. This was a problem because it directly conflicted with how we were raising our boys. The tensions were high, to say the least. Her mom always had some underhanded comment about how we were doing things, yet she never helped in any way. I was still working in Toledo at Western Auto, and Kris had transferred back to the Monroe Target.

As fate would have it, one day, I was looking in Kris's jewellery box for a ring that Kris wanted, and I guess she forgot about something she had written down and placed in there. There was a piece of paper with dates written on it, including when she had "been with" the "other man" and when she was with me. Apparently, she thought she may be pregnant and was trying to determine whose it was. Needless to say, my thoughts of an affair the night of the car accident were confirmed, and I was furious. I didn't even know how to react. I confronted her and then took off.

For the next several days, we were trying to figure out how to keep it all together.

If you have never learned how a metal is hardened, it is through heating and quenching known as heat treating. The metal is heated and quenched more than once, oftentimes. This process sets up the molecular structure to give the metal the desired strength and durability. There are many different types of heating and quenching methods, each of which is used for a particular outcome. This is similar in many ways to how God shapes and strengthens us for the particular calling He has for us. If the heating or quenching is not done right, the metal can turn too brittle or lack the desired hardness or formability. God, however, knows what He is doing as he sends us through His heat treatment to make us into the metal. He needs to do the job He needs us to do.

After spending a few days at a friend's house and cooling down, I came to my senses about what had to be done. She needed to come to repentance, and I needed to come to forgiveness. I returned home with the mindset that I was going to forgive no matter what. What I didn't know was that Kris had started a whole other battle with her sister in the meantime. Her sister did not like that Kris and I would not accept her son's behavior without correction and discipline being dealt with. Her sister had become irate about it, and it turned violent, very violent. In fact, her sister beat Kris up badly. She had a massive black eye and bruises all over her.

When I got home, I found her beaten and bruised, and I immediately knew what had happened. We kicked her sister out that day, and her mom and brother left as well.

Sometimes, the kingdom of God enters our lives forcefully, and all we can do is run to Jesus. As hard as that season was, it set a tone for Kris and me — it gave us a new determination to stick it out and find a way to restore our marriage. We realized the house was more than we needed, and the cost was straining us financially, so we broke the lease early and moved into an apartment in Monroe. After everything, I ended up battling another round of kidney infections. Meanwhile, the boys were growing up, wanting birthday parties and the normal joys of childhood.

The apartment life made it hard for us to do some things for the boys, and school days were fast approaching. We needed to get to a better school district. Through it, God kept us strong. I had one more procedure done on my kidney, which would become the last. I spent many hours in prayer, asking God to show me how to forgive and become the husband Kris needed me to be. Of course, He is always faithful, and healing is happening. He began to speak to me through Ephesians 5, where He talks about how a marriage looks like Christ and the church. I got this deep down in my spirit and began to apply it. There would be some struggles from time to time after this, but there was never any thought of divorce. We knew this would be till death do us part.

We didn't like the apartment building we were in, and something told me we needed to move. We wanted the boys to go to a smaller school so they could get a better education, but we had no money to put down on a house, and our credit at this point was not great.

One day, I was out looking around and found out about a module home park in Newport. They had several new homes and models to look at. We went and looked at one, and it was perfect. I started talking to the office about what we could do, and somehow, God moved the hearts of the people that were running the office. The lady I was working with asked me if we had anything at all that we would be willing to "trade in" for the down payment. The only thing I could think of was a set of Royal Prestige China we bought shortly after marriage. I showed her China, and she valued it enough for the down payment. We moved into that home for a set of China. About a month after we moved, a handicapped man who lived in the same apartment building we were in set his kitchen on fire.

Most of the buildings had to be evacuated, and a lot of people had to find a new place to live.

Doubling Down

1997, a new home, a new start! We were so excited to have the new house after going through so many trials. We knew that it was God and only God that had brought us through. The boys would attend a small country school, and we had a beautiful house in a park, yet out in the country. We were close to her dad and not too far from town. It was perfect! For the next 7 years, we would grow in faith, and our marriage would heal and become stronger than ever.

I wanted to get the boys into a church, and we all needed to go as a family, so I looked around at local churches and found Newport Community Church. We would attend that church for the next 15 years, and the boys would be baptized there. Kris was still working at Target, and I had found work at a local car dealership, making pretty good money now. By God's goodness and mercy, we were restored, and Kris conceived again that year. Through the process of forgiveness, God not only restored our marriage, but He healed me once and for all of the kidney issues that had plagued me for so long. Kris grew in her relationship with the Lord, and everything settled down.

1998, Andrew was born in April, the last of our three boys. At this point, everything was so good; I didn't want anything to change that. Satan never gives up, though, and a whole other trial is just around the corner. I thought we couldn't afford more children, so I had the procedure done to stop that from happening. That decision was not a good one; it actually haunted me for years, and I will elaborate on that later. The day Andrew and Kris came home from the hospital, the other two boys were playing in the yard, and tragedy struck.

Andrew was taking a nap, and Kris and I were resting. All of a sudden, we heard this blood-curdling scream out in the yard. I jumped up and ran to the front door to meet Tyler, zooming in and saying, "I didn't do it." Aaron was hot on his heels, blood spraying from his little hand. I ran back to the kitchen, grabbed a roll of paper towels, and ran back to the door to wrap up his hand to try and stop the bleeding. We all loaded up and rushed to the ER together. They were able to sew his finger back together, but that scar still remains.

Summer came, and the boys were playing in the yard, and life was good. I had come home from the dealership to have lunch with the family one summer day. Afterwards, Kris had some things to do in town, so we drove back into town in separate cars but together. I was looking over at the boys in the back of the van, and when I looked back in front of me, I saw a car stopped dead on the road. No lights or anything, just sitting right in front of me. I hit her doing like 50mph. The outcome was not good. I was life-flighted to the hospital, and my truck was towed to the storage yard. I was in the hospital for about a week with a very bad head injury and concussion.

When I came home, I was dizzy and had a lot of headaches for a long time. I had the truck moved to my father-in-law's house to stop paying storage and tried to go back to work too early. That resulted in more time off work. Bills got behind, and medical bills piled on. It didn't take too long to see where we were headed.

1999, we talked about it, prayed about it, thought about it, and finally decided that bankruptcy was the best option. It was hard to do that. Hard to see that we were in financial trouble again. We were able to keep the house, but our credit was ruined. I left the dealership world that year to work at the GM Powertrain plant, a job that Kris's uncle helped me get. This was a more stable income for us just when we needed it. At this point, we had been married for 7 years, had three children, and were both working pretty good jobs, but between the medical bills and having to replace the truck, we just couldn't make it. After filing, the lawyers took care of the rest, and we were free of some debt but burdened with the damaged credit. We had what we needed, so we learned to live on a cash-only budget. It didn't take long to feel like that was all behind us, but it really wasn't.

2000-2001, work and life continued without any major events. Some family relationships improved, like the one with my parents. In 2001, the World Trade Centers were hit, and the nation went on war footing. Life at our house was pretty good, however. We had plenty, and everything was getting paid. We were enjoying the kids now being in school, two of them anyway.

2002, Kris got fired from Target in the year. We felt it was a race discrimination case, but there was nothing to prove. She soon got a job at Cracker Barrel, which was, in some ways, a better position anyway. It certainly was a better company to work for. She worked there for three years.

2003, GM was going to force me to 2nd shift, something I didn't want to do with three young children in school. So I quit. There was an old paper factory in town where IKO had started a small paper line to make felt paper for roofing. I got a job there and quickly moved into a team lead position, which paid pretty well. Unfortunately, the company had some environmental concerns with the city of Monroe, and they didn't stay in Monroe long, 6 months or so. I think it is the only time in my life I collected unemployment. Of course, I couldn't do that for long either and ended up back at the dealership for a short time. Kris's cousin worked for the Detroit Free Press as a carrier and got a route for us there.

I would work for them for the next four years. Kris had begun to talk to me about going back to college, but I just couldn't see how I could make that happen with everything else going on, so I tried to table that, but it never went away as a topic. I was growing tired of living in the modular home park and wanted better for my family, so once again, I sought to make a deal with someone who could get us into a house.

There was a brand-new subdivision being built in Newport with pre-designed houses that you could customize within the builder's guidelines. I thought it looked nice and wanted to see if we could do something. To my surprise, they were able to get me a lender who would work with us despite the bankruptcy.

I should have known something was wrong but only saw a way to move up. We picked out a style and went through the particulars, and they built us a house. I think I knew the day we moved in that we were in trouble financially, but I figured we could overcome it.

At first, the payments were no more than what we had paid for the house in the park, and rent was manageable. Work at the dealership was going well at the time, so everything seemed fine. We were really living now! The kids loved it. Kris loved it. We finally had a real home that was ours.

But as life often goes, just when you think you've reached the top, something unexpected happens. The dealership business began to slow down, and since I was paid by the job and book time—not hourly—it had a serious impact on our income. To make ends meet, we started delivering papers for the *Detroit Free Press*, and before long, that became our main source of income. A large route opened up, I took it, and I said goodbye to being a mechanic for the last time. The paper route became a full-time job, but it wasn't well managed.

Over the next 4 years, I would grow the route to be a pretty good income for us, but the problem was proving all the income from it in a way that the banks would accept it. The ARM loan I had used to buy the house had matured and started adjusting to an interest rate that made it unaffordable and frankly not feasible. The bank did nothing to help me get to a fixed rate, which was no surprise there, so we ended up letting the house go. We moved out before the foreclosure hit our credit, which would make it very hard to get an apartment.

As hard as this was on all of us, I think it was hardest on my oldest so, who referred to our apartment as "living in the ghetto." There was a good outcome: the loss drove me to take my wife's counsel and go back to school.

Romans 8:28 – "All things work together for good for those who love God."

We often don't think of our spouse as a counselor, but we should. In fact, they can be the best counsel we can find. If we are married to a Godly spouse, He can use them to give us the best counsel we can receive. Kris had been telling me to go back to school, and this event finally woke me up to that. During our 7 years at the apartment, I finished a bachelor's degree, and it yielded a career that once and for all would end the financial struggles we had been in for 20 years. Before I could even finish, God would provide a solution. However, we had to go through one more bankruptcy before that came. We filed again in 2007, just 7 years after the first time. That would lock us up for 7 years. Once we went through those years, however, everything would change again.

2008-2009 - Once we settled into the apartment, we had little to do because we had no money. I started working two jobs again, the paper and a store manager at Midas for a year, and then from there, I worked at the Michelin tire warehouse.

I kept the paper route all through this till I knew Michelin was secure and had good enough pay. All during this time, I was also in school, taking 3 to 4 classes a semester to get through it as quickly as possible. Kris was looking for something different from Cracker Barrel, and she went to training to become a school bus driver and got hired at Jefferson Schools.

Something happened in our relationship there; we got closer, and somehow, our marriage improved even more. The level of trust and teamwork was high even in the hardship. We were still attending Newport Community church, and the boys were now moving into high school. In fact, Tyler was nearly done. He finished his last year at Airport School, but the other two boys had to move to Monroe School. It was hard on them, I know. I was busy all the time, attending school, doing homework, and working. Family time was slim, but we did the best we could. I graduated with my Associate's Degree with Honors from MCCC. I took a 3 plus 1 program with MCCC to complete my bachelor's at Eastern Michigan.

When I was near the end of my bachelor's degree, I began to pray and ask God to provide me with a job. One day, I was walking through the college and saw flyers everywhere offering lessons to learn how to fly and obtain a pilot's license. God told me you need to meet this man to take the lessons. I had no money to pay for them, so I asked my sister to pray with me about it, and she offered to help. She also told my parents, who offered to help pay for it. I started the lessons by finding out that this man was a Christian man and an engineer for Chrysler in Dundee. During one of our lessons, as we were flying, he said if I was looking for work, he could probably get me in at Chrysler. I applied, and not only did I get a job, but I got interviewed for his position. It turned out that he was leaving to join the Air Force as a pilot. I literally stepped right into his position. I doubled my pay on day one, and it continued growing into a paycheck that launched us into a different life.

In 2010, I graduated from Eastern Michigan with a Bachelor's Degree with honors. My mom and dad were able to attend my graduation from Eastern. Though Dad never endorsed college and had not finished high school himself, he was proud of me that day. Dad had never said anything to me about how he treated me when I was younger and sick with my kidney issues. Still, he finally came to me with an apologetic tone and said he never knew how sick I really was, and he was sorry for how he had treated me back then. He had battled cancer a couple of times by now, and it took a lot out of him. The cancer would return shortly after that, and he passed away in October 2011. Even though Dad and I had never really seen eye to eye on a lot of things, I will say he was a good man. He was a Godly man who did the best he could have done with his understanding. He taught me to love the Lord and to always give my best shot. He worked hard to raise 10 children, and he and his mom were blessed.

2012 - No sooner than clearing the bankruptcy did we start looking for a house again. We had cleaned up the financial mess and were ready to start again. We were driving old cars with no payments, and it was the best time to buy a house before we needed new cars. Kris had seen a house in town and wanted to look into it, so she told me about it. It was a bank-owned/foreclosure and had just been listed again. We contacted a realtor and looked at it. It needed a lot of work, but it was in a good neighborhood and had good bones. It was a huge house. With two sons now getting ready to leave for the Army, we didn't think we really needed all that, but it seemed like a very good investment opportunity. So, we started looking for a lender. The roof on the house needed to be replaced before an insurance company would even talk to us about it. There were some deals that had to be made, but we could get the house cheap. I went to an old high school friend to get insurance to get through closing, but the bank made me have a contract set up with a roofing contractor to get it replaced. The insurance was astronomically priced, but I would only need it till the roof was done. We were able to make all of the deals and get a great fixed-rate loan. The house would become a 7-year project, but it was so big that we didn't mind.

This time, it was right. We had more than enough income, and the house had a lot of potential to grow in value with some work. The next seven years were often referred to as the "Camelot" years. We closed on the house in May and had the summer to move in. I immediately went about fixing things that needed it.

At this point, I would like to take a break from the chronological storyline and talk about some of the ways that by applying God's Word, we were able to overcome some terrible things along the way. Revelation 12:11 tells us that they (meaning the saints) overcame him (meaning Satan) by the blood of the Lamb and the word of their testimony. The blood of the Lamb is quite easy to understand, that is to say, Jesus's sacrifice on the cross so that we may be forgiven. The word of their testimony, however, takes a little closer look. What exactly is your testimony? It is an account of your life, of what Jesus has done for you personally, but it is also an account of what you have done. What we do for the Lord, for others, and for ourselves is our testimony. Your acts are a statement of what you believe in. It is more than just a story we tell about what God has done for us. By living a life that is determined by God's direction, we show that we have faith in Him, and we believe that He will be faithful to what He has said. Perhaps of all the things we can do, forgiveness is one of the biggest keys that God gives us to unlock our freedom to overcome things that burden us in our lives.

For example, the kidney issues I dealt with for so many years, with doctor visit after doctor visit and procedure after procedure. Finally, all went away when I was able to fully forgive Kris for the unfaithfulness that she fell into years after the kidney problems started. I realized that I, too, shared some responsibility for that and was able to forgive myself as well. Forgiving can unlock all sorts of blessings from God. Physical healing, financial freedom, relationship healing, and more. Forgiveness is a powerful tool that should be exercised regularly, often, and quickly. Matthew 6:14-15, Colossians 3:13, Ephesians 4:32, Leviticus 19:18, and Matthew 18:21-22 speak on the commandment to forgive. The rewards of forgiveness are self-evident and undeniable, as seen from a medical standpoint, a financial standpoint, and a mental health standpoint. Basically, your life depends upon your ability to forgive. So, forgive yourself and others often.

Another way to overcome things is by following good Godly counsel. As I mentioned, a spouse's advice is often overlooked as "Godly counsel" but is often where we receive the best counsel if our spouse is a Godly person. Think about it: who knows you better than your spouse? Who knows how you think and react, how you plan and spend money and time, and just everything about you? Your spouse knows what the needs of the household are. They know what the strengths of the household are. They know your strengths and weaknesses. We ought to pray daily for our spouses and ask God how to counsel them regarding the decisions they face. And when we receive counsel from them, we would do wise to follow or at least very strongly consider their counsel.

When Kris told me I needed to get back into school, I weighed that advice carefully and prayerfully. I knew she was right, but I had to wait for God's timing to do it. She didn't stop offering that advice because I didn't immediately respond. She just kept saying it with kindness and encouragement until it happened. Husbands, I think this is especially important for you as we tend to think that men are to be the leaders in the house, and I think that to be true, but understand that when your wife speaks to you with counsel, she is speaking from a place of knowing. Proverbs 31 10-11, 26 says it well.

10 – "Who can find a virtuous woman? For her price is far above rubies." 11 – "The heart of her husband doth safely trust in her so that he shall have no need of spoil." 26 – "She openeth her mouth with wisdom; and in her tongue is the law of kindness."

Prayer time and making our petitions known to God is another key to overcoming. We often don't spend enough time praying before making decisions or facing a life trial. We try to "do it alone" before we decide that "all we can do now is pray." Prayer is the fragrance that turns God's head, and he hears our prayers and can and will intercede on our behalf more than we can possibly imagine. When the answer is delayed, or the answer is no, we often think our prayer has gone "unanswered" when, in fact, God is saying wait for my timing, or I have something better in mind for you than what you are asking for.

Our testimony is that often, God answered my prayer and granted me what I asked for. But how often do we give God praise when He says to wait or that He has a different plan for us? Overcoming is knowing that God is on the throne, He is always answering prayers, and no matter what the answer is, we give Him praise for it.

2013 - I moved to Trenton Engine with Chrysler following a promotion and began working on a Master's Degree in Engineering Management.

Kris was still driving the school bus, and our two older boys were now in the Army, the oldest one being married now. He got married at Newport Community Church. The reception was held in our backyard under a tent we rented. The house is coming along very nicely at this point, and Kris wants a swimming pool. I was looking through the paper one day and saw someone's ad that was giving away a Kayak pool for free; you just had to go take it down. So, I did just that. Aaron was in El Paso, TX, during his whole time in the Army. We were able to fly down to see him there. The day after Aaron got home from El Paso, after leaving the Army, we used the trailer he rented to get his Jeep home to go get the pool. We went and took it down, and I started prepping to set it up in our yard. I had to put up a fence around the yard, bury two overhead electrical wires in the house, and set up the electrical service for the filter pump. I pulled the permits from the city and got to work. I got the pool put up before the spring of 2014 opening season.

2014 - I graduated from my Master's program, and we had a summer of celebration. Tyler and Charlotte came home for leave, and we went up to Mackinac Island, a vacation spot we often frequented when the kids were younger. On the way home, we stopped at a boat sales place and looked at a new boat. We went up a couple of days later to pick up a Yamaha AR 192. We had so much family fun on that boat over the next several years, fishing, tubing, cruising the hot hole, and more. The pool was beautiful, and the house and yard were wonderful as well. It truly was the Camelot years. At Christmas time, we decorated the house with lights, two trees, and a village. The wood burner never stopped burning in the winter, and the house was beautiful at this point.

2015-2016: We hosted the family Christmas at our house and had a full house. My mom, all my siblings, their kids, and even some of Kris's family came. Everyone enjoyed Santa Claus coming and handing out gifts. It was so fun to host the big family Christmas party in our home. We were still attending church every week at Newport Community Church, and I led the music and sang in the choir. Kris enjoyed having summers off work, spending time in the pool, and reading.

Winter 2015-2016 was hard. We had a lot of snow and ice. Driving to work was a challenge, and many times, I took back roads to avoid the expressway backups. Kris bought Christmas gifts for some of the kids on her bus. With hats, gloves, and blankets, we helped a couple of families in need with a few things. We had finally gotten to a very comfortable place in life. Kris, I had time to travel and see the boys where they were stationed. Tyler was in Maryland for a while, and then he went to Georgia.

The Accident

2017 is the year that will live in infamy in our family history. The year of the great fall. The year had started just as 2015 and 16 were. Things were continuing to go well. We drove new cars and enjoyed the house, pool, and boat. It seemed we had finally gotten to a "normal" place. Work was going well, with new projects coming all the time, plenty of growth, and opportunity to advance. Kris enjoyed her year of bus driving as always. Andrew was finishing high school, and the older boys were still off in the Army. Summer was in full swing when Tyler got to come home for his leave.

He and Charlotte stayed at our house for a week or two while they worked on the house they had bought. I had wanted to cut down a tree in the backyard but couldn't do it on my own, so I thought Tyler could help me one day. But they were busy doing the things they wanted to do, so I decided to try to get it done on my own. Their neighbor came out to help, but something went wrong.

I was up in the tree about 30 feet off the ground, trimming out some limbs, when all of a sudden, everything went black. The next thing I knew, a couple of fire department guys were trying to get me onto a stretcher. I was rushed to Toledo Hospital and don't remember the next three days.

When I finally woke up, I realized I had had a very nasty spill. I was in a hospital bed with people gathered around looking at me. How bad is it, I wondered? I couldn't really even feel myself yet. It almost felt like I wasn't really there.

Apparently, the prognosis was not good, as I would find out later myself. I had fallen out of the tree and landed on the concrete driveway. I broke seven vertebrae in my back, my left shoulder was shattered, and I had a very nasty skull fracture that nearly killed me. I couldn't really feel any of that yet. The doctors had speculated that I wouldn't make it through the first night. Then they said I would most likely never walk again. There was talk of putting pins and rods in my back and the possibility of an impaired mental state.

I remember my boss, Aaron, my son, and Kris being there. Aaron stated that on his one-night watch, he witnessed me get up, go to the bathroom, and come back to bed all on my own. Of course, my own memory of any of that is fuzzy at best. I was in the hospital for a couple of weeks and then finally released to go home without so much as one surgery. I could not move my left arm, and I had no sense of taste or smell. I could not hear out of my left ear. I could barely walk, but I could walk. I went home, and I didn't leave the living room for the next couple of months. I slept and ate and laid on the couch for two months.

At this point, Aaron, Andrew, his wife, Kara, and their new baby (Liam) were living at home, and Tyler had signed up for an extended service of 2 years, so Charlotte was living with us as well. Kris was not handling the fact that my condition may render me incapable of returning to work well at all. I was receiving a full paycheck at this point and had disability coverage, which was very, very good. We were not hurting financially. Thank God for that.

Physical therapist started coming to the house to help me start rehabilitating, and we started with my shoulder. I was also seeing a specialist for it, and he believed that surgery of any kind was a last resort, which I was glad to hear. He was working closely with my back doctor to come up with a program to help me heal. He prescribed ultrasonic therapy for my shoulder fractures, which seemed to be having a hard time healing on their own. And physical therapy to regain my range of motion. The insurance company didn't want to pay for the ultrasonic therapy, so he had to fight to get it, but he was able to get it. The physical therapy was so painful it was hard to do at first. Everything had grown so tight it just didn't want to move.

On top of that, I lost an enormous amount of muscle mass and was very weak. Life was about pain at that point, but I was just happy to be alive and able to work on getting better. The accident happened on 6 August, the day before my birthday. We had been at the Monroe County Fair the day before, where we saw a work colleague of mine. He said when he heard what happened, he could not believe it. It would take me 7 months of physical therapy and a lot of time in prayer and seeking God to return to work.

During this time, I spent a lot of time praying and seeking God's guidance on what I should do from here. At first, I did not know if I would be able to return to work, and there were a lot of questions about that. Kris was very concerned and started to make some moves to be in a position to replace my income should that be needed. I never really understood what a toll this was taking on her till years later. What we didn't know then was that God had begun to set the stage for major changes in our lives.

At this point, we had been married for 25 years, raised three children, owned two houses, earned college degrees, and had finally gotten into successful careers. It seemed as though all of that was teetering on a knife edge now. What if I can't return to work? Will we lose the house? Will Kris be able to make it on her own? Are the boys able to make it on their own yet? These were the hours of my prayers. It had started to turn cold now, and firewood needed to be moved every day. I often found myself carrying in wood under a tremendous amount of pain at a very slow rate while watching my sons sit on their butts, and Kris was taking care of our dogs and Charlotte's dogs. We felt unappreciated and used, and it finally got to me one day. I was yelling about the kids not helping and not paying the small amount we had asked them to help pay the bills. Charlotte got mad and moved out the next day. This was the beginning of the end of Camelot.

Kris decided to take a shot at a new job to make sure we would be okay. A friend of hers worked for Chrysler and gave her a referral to get an hourly position. Once she applied, I talked to the HR people at the plant where she was interviewed, and she got in at Warren Truck. She quit bus driving and went to work on the assembly line. She didn't work for very long before getting very sick. She had her 90 days in, so they held her job, but she was off because she was sick and transferred up to Flint, MI. This was about an hour and 15 minutes' drive from home on a good day.

By this time, I knew that I was going to be able to return to work, so I told her to just quit and ask if she could get back to bus driving. She did, but she was now at the bottom of the seniority ladder and had to be in a substitute position. She did not like it at all.

Meanwhile, while all of this was going on, God had started to speak to me about leaving Chrysler and going in a direction He was calling me to go, which was to start a farm. Now, remember we live in downtown Monroe, and I currently work up at Trenton Engine. Those two things are not conducive to starting a farm. I knew right away I would have to sell the house. But it was so strong within me to act on what God was telling me that I couldn't wait. So, I went out and bought a tractor and equipment to start farming hay. I had no fields, no idea how to get to a field, or anything at all. I just knew if I started moving, God would, too. Tyler, my oldest son, had the money to buy the tractor, I had the money to buy a baler and sickle bar mower, and Aaron, my middle son, bought a hay rake.

2018, during the year it took to acquire the equipment, I was working 70-80 a week to get the house ready to sell. Coming right out of 7 months off work and in rehab, to working 70-80 a week and then working on a house, all the while collecting equipment to do something that I knew next to nothing about. My dad had a small hobby farm where I learned a small amount about animals and caring for them, but that was 35 years ago, and I was very young. Now, I was going to own it and call the shots.

I went to my boss, mentor, and friend and talked to him about what I was planning to do. He had been watching me and helping me rise up through the ranks at Chrysler, and he was at my bedside in the hospital. He had promoted me time and time again, and now I was asking him for his blessing to leave the company and start a farm. He said, "You mean like a full working farm?" I said, "Yes, Mike," and showed him pictures of the farm equipment I had bought.

Now, the reason I worked so hard for the year 2018 was to help him get a product launch that had gone very far in the wrong direction back on track and producing at a rate. He was the plant manager at Trenton at the time, and it was important to his career that this be a success. So, I asked him to return the favor and let me transfer back to Dundee, a more rural area, so I could be closer to farmland where I could find a farm to buy and run. So, he granted my request and let me go.

We sold the Lincoln Camelot house in May of 2019, exactly 7 years after we bought it, and made $105,000 more than we bought it for. We bought an old farmhouse built in 1910. It was an old dairy farm, and the land had been sold off, so all we got was the house and two acres. Here's where God's plan really starts going. Before we moved, a friend of mine from the Dundee Engine plant said he was looking for a farmer to take care of his 10-acre hay crop. I told him I was looking for some land to farm and had shared my story with him. I agreed to farm his land and pay him for it. So, we started cutting hay right away from the house in Monroe. We drove the tractor and equipment all the way across Monroe County to get to his place to farm 10 acres. The field was so overgrown that year that my equipment could barely cut it, and balancing it was not easier, but we got it done. We sold that crop to a horse farm way up north of Monroe and had to haul it up there.

2019 - No one, and I mean no one, in their right mind, would look at what I was doing and think, "This guy is one smart dude." My neighbors thought I was nuts. Kris was not happy at all about selling the house, and there is a whole other story to tell on that, but for this one, let's just say there was a battle that had to be won. When we moved, we had no help. It was Kris, Aaron, and me. We loaded and unloaded the U-Haul van three times and a trailer two more times after that. We moved in May, and I opened Wingate Stables LLC in June.

At this point, I really had no intention of leaving Chrysler anytime soon and thought, God, you're going to have to do something miraculous to make this farm something we can live off of. Little did I know He had some changes coming that would turn my world upside down and make me reconsider everything I thought I knew up to that point, but that will come later. Those first years, I was still healing from the tree accident, and my body hurt everywhere. I had constant problems with my left ear. Infections and draining and no hearing. Tyler and I had some differences of opinion, and he needed the tractor he had bought for his farm, so I had to buy another one.

There ended up being some divisions in the family, and Kris, Tyler, and Andrew had a bad falling out. So now this farm has Kris, Aaron, and me running it. The house needed work. The barn needed work, and the equipment needed work. The house had a pool, which was good for Kris. She had left the workforce altogether at this point and was helping me to start this farm. She would drive the tractor while I stacked bales of hay. She took care of the animals while I was at work. She helped in so many ways. She started canning from the garden and bottle-fed animals.

In 2020, we started out with two young heifers we planned to raise for beef. Then we added pigs and, finally, chickens. The pig project was a joint venture with my siblings so they could all get to try the first fruits of the farm. I raised six pigs that year, and it turned out great. We were doing it! We were farming! I had a plan to grow the farm over the next 10 years or so, hopefully be able to get some more land somehow, and make it into a job. But when God says He wants you to do something, things happen that we don't plan in a timeline we can't imagine. It took us a year to settle things into the house, though that would never happen. It got to a level where we felt comfortable.

Aaron was living with us, and I was working to get him into his house. He finally was able to buy a house and get moved in before the end of the year. I started having a lot of trouble with my left ear with drainage and ear infections. I got so bad one night that I drove myself to urgent care. I had been seeing a specialist for the draining, and they had run some tests, but he kept telling me there was little they could do and I was going to have to live with it.

After that night, I went to a new doctor, who referred me to the Michigan Ear Institute. I made an appointment there and saw the doctor. He looked at my ear and said they had been treating me for the wrong thing. He put some medicine in my ear and told me he could fix not only the reason I had gotten the infections but also the draining and loss of hearing I had since the accident of 2017. One surgery, and it was all fixed!

Tragedy and Trial

Two thousand twenty-one with all of the issues, but my teeth were now fixed from the accident, and I was starting to feel pretty good again. That summer was good. Kris and I were having a very good year. Things with the boys were still not good, but I figured in time that would heal, too. We had a garden and had bought some more cattle. We now had a pair of pigs that produced a lovely litter of babies. Kris was starting to embrace the farm life more and more.

Driving the tractor and working in the garden, it seemed the transition to farm life was going very well. I was working continuously on improving the farm in all kinds of ways. Kris was planting things all over the yard, and we were enjoying the peace and quiet of country life and learning how it felt to be empty nesters.

That fall, COVID-19 was still in full swing; they had been threatening to require the vaccines to stay employed, and for a time, they had shut everything down. We worked from home as best we could for a while, but there was little to do with the plant being shut down. Kris was spending more and more time with her friend Christine and had asked me several times to help her get some things done around her house. Christine's husband had passed away several years ago, and she was a

54

widow. There were a lot of things that needed a man's attention around the house. Kris's mom was ill and in the hospital in Monroe, and Kris went up several times to see her there.

At the beginning of November, Kris started getting ill. We didn't suspect anything major at first, but she steadily got worse. I was feeling somewhat under the weather but still okay to go to work, which had resumed by then. However, I was still under a very close watch for COVID-19. We had to verify that we didn't have COVID-19 every day and had to wear masks all day. Kris had gotten so sick I decided to take some time off work to be at home with her.

Finally, she was so weak she couldn't get up to move around. I took her to the hospital that night, not understanding how serious things were. I called the hospital en route, and they said to bring her to the ER doors. I dropped her off, and before I could park the truck and get back inside, they had taken her to the back and had an oxygen mask on her. Now she was so weak she really couldn't talk anymore.

In just two weeks, she went from working in the yard to not being able to talk from being so weak. They came in and told me they needed to do a chest x-ray. So, they brought the machine right into the room where we were and allowed me to see the image as it came up. As soon as I saw it, I knew she was in deep trouble. Her lungs were completely full of fluid. They told me they would need to put her into a coma and onto a ventilator. I didn't know what to do. I looked at her, and she looked back at me. She just smiled with the most peaceful smile I think I have ever seen her wear. I just knew, somehow, this was it. This would be the last time I would see her. They left the room for us to say goodbye. I kind of knew this would be the last goodbye, but it wasn't real; this couldn't really be happening. I went home that night in complete shock.

The next day, I called work and told them what was going on, and I had to go test for COVID myself since I was exposed to her. Of course, I tested positive, too, but I just felt run down, nothing like what she was going through. They put me on short-term disability, and I spent the next week in shock. I couldn't see her because she was in isolation. Of course, I told all of the family what was going on, but no one could come to see me because I also had COVID.

Every day, I would get up, feed the animals, get a fire going, and sit there staring out the window in disbelief. I called the hospital twice daily for updates; they gave me enough reason to hope, but it was not good news either. Finally, after a week, they said I could see her. So, I went up, and she looked like she was already gone. Her body was there, and the machine was breathing for her, but she was gone. I told the kids they needed to come see her, but I didn't tell them just how bad it was. Only Aaron came, only once. Every day for the next 10 days, I went to sit by her bedside and wait. Wait for something; I watched the oxygen levels and all the machines, hoping. But it was over. The doctor came to talk to me. He told me that there were only days left, and they would have to take her off the ventilator. I told the kids to come and say goodbye. They couldn't do it.

On 28 November, they took her off the machines. My brother was there to support me. We prayed together, read scriptures to her, and watched as she drew her last breaths, but she was already gone. She had left the night I dropped her off before they ever put her on the ventilator. God took her in His mighty arms and accepted her into the home He had already prepared just for her.

If 2017 was the equivalent of Star Wars: A New Hope, then 2021 was The Empire Strikes Back. For the next week after Kris passed away, I spent my time planning a funeral and talking with family. I did all of the planning. The boys and their wives came to one meeting at the funeral home to pick out a casket and go over a few things. I wrote and delivered the eulogy, and my brother followed with a few words. There was a very large turnout of support at the showing and funeral service, and that was goodbye. I spent the next week in silence. My mom had been sick for the last month, and she was now in a nursing home and not doing well. I went down to see her; she was not well. She asked about Kris and the funeral, and she was sorry for my loss. About a week later, they moved her to my sister's house for her final few days. I went to see her a couple of times, and we sang songs with her before she passed away, just 22 days after Kris had died. I took some more time off work. I just couldn't function.

Kris's friend Christine, whom I had been doing some work for around her house, was taking Kris's passing very hard. I was talking quite a bit with her, and I thought something might be happening. I was not built to be alone, and she was a widow, too. I thought we might have some things in common.

After having her over to my house along with her daughter for Christmas and meeting my sons, I thought things might go in the same direction. I guess for her, I was just a shoulder to cry on for a while and someone who could help her through a rough spot here and there. She was very strange and very withdrawn. After a little while, I realized this was not a good relationship and broke it off.

A New Beginning

2022 - It has been just over a month, and I somehow made it through the holidays. I still am not back to work and had no idea how I was going to make that happen. I had hit a really low spot, and I saw no way forward. I was trying to reach out to find support, but was struggling to find what I needed.

One weekend, I sat by my wood burner for three days straight, staring out the window with a cup of coffee in my hand, praying some but mostly waiting. Waiting for God to speak. I told God that if He wanted me to do this farm thing, I could not do it alone; in fact, I could not do life alone. I didn't want to. I just wasn't built to be alone. What I got back was a question. "Why do you need a wife?' I said, "I need a helper; I need support," He said, "Then you need to seek the right kind of woman." I know, I know, you're thinking, man, he's only been a widow for just over a month, and he can't handle it?

It wasn't a question of my capability; I was an engineering manager for Chrysler. At this point, I had next to no bills. I was self-supporting. I knew how to cook, do laundry, and take care of the animals. The real thing is this: I didn't want to do it alone. What purpose was there in it for me?

I had bought tickets to go to a play-up in Detroit at the Fox Theater for Oklahoma to show on 16 February, but now it seems I had no one to go with me. I was thinking through who I might ask to go when I came across Sue L., who was now Sue W.

She had found out through Christine, oddly enough, that my wife was very ill with COVID-19 and contacted me the day Kris passed away. She had been checking in on me from time to time since that day to see how I was doing. We had been talking quite a bit. She was divorced, but it seemed to me that she was still trying to figure out if there was some way they might be able to work things out, so I felt I didn't want to intrude. But as the conversations continued, it seemed there was just no way. So, I thought, what the heck? I will ask her. Sue and I had gone to high school together and were in the same group of friends, but I was having all the kidney issues back in those days. I was very withdrawn and shy and didn't really talk to the girls too much.

After high school, we went our separate ways for 30 years. But now here we were, talking like old friends. She accepted the invitation to go, and I picked her up at her house that day.

The date started out great. The venue was so nice, and we had a good conversation on the way there. The play started out a little strange but not too far off from something normal. It quickly went south. The play ended up being some new age, very liberal representation of the original Oklahoma, and it got so bad that we ended up getting up and walking out in the middle of it. We had a nice dinner in a small restaurant in downtown Monroe. We had a nice time, and things took off pretty fast from there. In fact, they went extremely fast.

I had my house on the market to sell, but I had just given up on selling and pulled it off the market. The next day, I got an almost full offer. I accepted the offer, and things started kicking into high gear. I started to think about whether or not to buy another house or just sell everything and move to an apartment. Sue had another plan, and apparently, so did God. Sue and her daughter were working on a flip house, and she had asked me to come over and take a look at it. I went over and soon got involved in helping to finish it. That one was pretty much done, and they had a second one that needed some minor electrical work, so I also went there.

Our lives were quickly coming together, and soon, we were looking at a new farm that was bigger than the one I had by quite a bit. It needed a lot of work, but that didn't scare Sue.

By this time, a few weeks had gone by, and we were in full swing of dating. We submitted an offer on the new farm and started making plans to get married. I came through the first part of the hurricane of the accident in 2017, through the passing of my wife and mom in 2021. There was a brief eye of the storm where things quieted down just a little with some time off work, but now, I was on the other side and headed into the more powerful backside of the storm. No sooner than the first flip house sold, Emily, Sue's daughter, and I looked at another house to flip and decided to make an offer.

It is now the end of April 2022, and Sue and I have an accepted offer on the farm. We had started planning a wedding and were getting ready to move my house into the new farmhouse. In April, we decided to buy a new, bigger tractor that could handle the bigger farm. After looking around for a while, we decided on one that was out in West Virginia.

So far, we have taken a few road trips to get more cattle and make plans for the new growing farm. We set a date for the wedding for 7 May, and low and behold, the closing on the farm came back on 9 May. The new flip house offer was accepted, and we decided to get going on that as soon as possible. So even though the backside of the hurricane is a whole different type of energy than the destructive front, it is a storm of activity nonetheless.

The Scripture says that God will not let the flames of fires come upon you nor the waters to overflow you. There are two very different types of trials in life, either of which can destroy you if you do not have God to shield you. I think of fire as something that burns and consumes you, whereas a flood of water can overtake or overfill and drown you. It is important to understand that you need God to shield you in either case.

Satan can come at you in so many ways, tempting you in loss and in great gain. At this moment, I felt like plenty of each was dished up on my plate, sufficient to sink any ship if the Lord was not at the helm.

7 May has arrived, and many who are close to me have had trouble understanding what I was doing and why I was moving so fast. When God spoke to me during my time off after the accident, He set a fire in me to see this farm happen regardless of the cost. I didn't know that everything He was doing from that moment on was preparing me for this. Sue and I closed on the new farm on 9 May. In order to buy the farm with the acreage, the banks required an agricultural loan. To qualify for those loans, a person has to show that they have experience in farming and the equipment to do it.

If God had not started me out on the small farm Kris and I had, Sue and I could not have bought this new farm. Sue had tried to buy a farm before and ran into this problem. I couldn't have bought the farm on my own either, as I didn't have enough income to show.

It took the two of us bringing our experiences and careers together to get it done. God promised to cover me and keep me even when things got dark, and they did for a while. Now was the time to move, and we did move. We got married, closed on the farm, and began moving into the farm. We quit our corporate jobs and went on to do what God was calling us to do. Sue and I were like two storms merging into one. The amount of chaos that would result was staggering.

We had flip houses going. Emily and Sue had decided to buy a church building that was going to be remodeled into a home (more on that later), and we were trying to get the new farmhouse livable (more on that in a minute), and then there was the farm itself getting animals moved and settled in, and we still both had corporate jobs at the start. I moved into Sue's house until we could get the farmhouse ready to move into, and we kept the corporate jobs going until we could figure out how the new picture would look.

Chrysler asked me to go to the Kokomo, IN plant to assist with a new engine line they were trying to launch there. It hadn't been going well, and they needed help. I asked if Sue could go with me, and they allowed her to come. We spent a week out there, and she worked remotely from the hotel while I was at the plant each day. That was the closest thing we would get to a honeymoon, so we thought we had better take advantage of it.

After a week of thinking about things from afar, I think we both understood what needed to happen, but it was a scary deal. With the farm, the flip house, and the church all going at once, there was just no way I could stay at Chrysler anymore. And besides, God had told me He wanted to use my talents elsewhere, and it had become clear where that was. I left Chrysler one month after we got married, and Sue left her job a couple of weeks later.

That summer, we spent our days working on the flip house and working to get the farmhouse ready to live in. It needed a new well, a new septic tank, and a leach field; the plumbing to the bathroom upstairs was not working, and the downstairs was only a half bath. The kitchen needed a lot of work, and when we started to dig into things, the list just got longer, as it most often does. At first, traveling back and forth from the farm to Sue's house, aka Jackman, was fine because it wasn't that far, and the animals were adjusting to their new home, and there weren't so many of them yet.

However, as the summer went on, we continued to rapidly add to the number of cattle. We were picking up cattle at least twice a month, three or four heads at a time. We were up to about 30 by the end of that first summer and there was a lot of pressure on the fences. We had also moved Sue's horse Jack to the farm from the boarding stable where he was and got him a friend, Charlie. We had a pig and some chickens as well.

Fall 2022 - We finished the flip house, and it was sold before Christmas. We were on a trip down south, about 8 hours away, picking up some cattle, and we got a call that our cattle were out. I had to call my brother to go over to the farm to get them rounded up. This wasn't the first time, but the frequency was getting worse and worse. By the time winter came, the neighbors were becoming very sore with us, and we needed to do something. That winter was a very difficult one. We had decided to move into the farmhouse, which still had no heat and no functioning shower or laundry.

Winter 2022-2023 - I had worked very hard all summer to get some source of heat into the house, and just before the worst cold hit, we finally got a wood burner installed and hooked up. We had little to no firewood, but God provided it, and we were able to pick up a bunch of free wood from someone close by. The wood was all very large and needed to be slit, but we had some heat. The house was a complete disaster inside.

We had mountains of stuff everywhere in every room. Trying to figure out how to become organized while staying functional in the chaos was a huge challenge. With no shower or laundry, we had to go over to the Jackman house to shower and wash clothes. The cattle escaping was still a problem, and we ended up getting a ticket before we could get some new fencing put in and slow down the bleeding.

By then, it had been decided that the church would not be a good flip to a home, and Sue's dad recommended it just remain a church and be rented for weddings and such. So now it was to become a commercial venue. That venture was started with little to no understanding of what was required to be a commercial rental property. So, there were a lot of hurdles to overcome to make this all happen. Money was quickly becoming tight, and with no more corporate money coming in, something had to be done. It was clear that the flip house money would be tied up in the venue for some time, and

Jackman was not selling, though it had not been on the market a long time.

We were beginning to think some work would have to be done to get it to sell. We were carrying two mortgages, the farm was bleeding money, and the venue was far from being able to rent to anyone for anything.

That Christmas, we had a Wingate family Christmas party at the venue because my brother was looking for a place to have it, and we needed the money to rent it. It was not ready. We had set up a makeshift kitchen and serving area upstairs in the main room and set up a bunch of tables to set up food on. We plugged in several crockpots and warming trays to heat and keep food warm. When the electrical system started trying to handle all of this, it quickly became clear that it needed to be upgraded. Breakers kept blowing, and some of the food ended up being cold. It was a good party, though, and everyone enjoyed it.

As 2023 started, we got a shower hooked up at the farm, and the wood burner was keeping us warm. The animals continued needing to be watched closely as we could not work on the fencing till the weather got better. We had to buy a lot of hay that winter because we had grown the herd faster than we had grown our capacity to feed them.

Sue decided to go back to work and get a job in the corporate world. So now she would be juggling that again.

After the Christmas party, we got to work on the church, remodeling it into a wedding venue. The upstairs had to be gutted and bathrooms added, and the basement kitchen was complete overall, with everything from new cabinets to adding a bathroom and upgrading the electrical service. It took us until the end of the summer of 2023 before we were ready to open.

In spring 2023, we started off the farming season with some added fields and calves that were born over the winter. We had lost a couple of calves in the cold, but the ones that made it, were doing very well. We ended up with eight calves, and we had gotten some feeder pigs with the hopes that one would be breedable, but she didn't work out. Some things on the farm work out, and some don't. You just have to keep working and trusting that God will provide. The farm needed so much cleanup work done, and we were working so much just to keep it running and improving along the way; it had definitely become a full-time job at that point for two people, not just one. With Sue working and trying to complete the venue, it is quite amazing that we had time for a few getaways here and there. Some trips up north to a cabin and even one trip to the Caribbean for a week. God is faithful, and He gives us time to rest when we need it, and we definitely need it.

With Jackman Rd house on the market, it seemed that we were getting very close to being through the backside of the 7-year hurricane we had been in. We started out this season, each of us in our own situation, but when God brought us together mid-way through, things just got even crazier. In the first couple of years Sue and I were married; it seemed so much had changed for me that I was no longer even the same person.

2024 - With each day that passes now, things get better. We have come through a massive storm in life, and a new day is dawning. The air seems cleaner somehow when we go to feed the livestock in the morning. The sun seems to shine a little brighter as though the ones that have gone on before us are smiling down to give us a better day. As the Psalms says, God has been rich in His blessings, and mercies are new every morning.

As I sit on this cold December morning and reflect back on the year 2024, I see God's handiwork all over our lives. He has given grace when we need it, and when we have cried, He is there. There are more good days now than bad ones as we climb further away from the storm. We bought a brand-new tractor this year after ours broke down last fall, harvesting corn silage. We also bought a new hay baler.

So, this year's hay season was a vast improvement over any before. God was faithful to provide enough hay this year to last us until the next hay season as our herds and flocks continue to grow. Our customers have been good to us this year, supporting us and being good neighbors. Some other things going on this year were the parking lot improvements and events that happened at the venue.

Things have settled down with the township, and bookings are increasing all the time. Sue has been working very hard to market both the venue and the farm and is doing a fantastic job of growing both. I couldn't have imagined a better woman. Sue is a rock, and she cares so much about me. God truly fashioned her just for me and brought us together in His own perfect way and with His own perfect timing.

Overcoming is so much more than just making it through trials and tribulations. It is a growing discipleship with our heavenly Father, who, in His own ways, grows us and makes us better than we could have ever imagined ourselves to be able to come. When we go through trials, we need to press into God at those times, not just to survive but to grow. We see things in nature grow through some of the most harsh conditions. This morning, it was 13 degrees out, and I was out feeding the cows. We have a couple of calves that are a month and 2 months old. They were both running, playing, and loving life. I am sure they like the warm summer air better with fresh grass to feed on, but they do not slow down during the winter.

24 December, Christmas Eve morning. Sue and I took a rest this morning and some time to just slow down and reflect on what has happened in the past year—things we have accomplished, things God has done in our lives, troubles we had, and how we came through it all. We talked about the new year coming and, things we'd like to see happen, goals we want to accomplish, and ways that we can strengthen relationships.

During this discussion, I began to realize that Kris and I did not take time to do this nearly enough, nor to the depth that Sue and I are in. It is so important, however, to do this. I wonder how many marriages fail because these very open, honest, and candid discussions do not happen at all. One of the biggest things that Sue and I came up with in order to make these discussions happen is that there has to be a few things agreed upon.

First and foremost, trust has to be a cornerstone of any meaningful relationship. I am not talking about trusting someone not to cheat on you with another person. This kind of betrayal only happens after the little things are already abandoned. It's the trust that when something is said, it is said out of love. It is the trust that when one person is having a difficult day, the other is doing everything they can to make it better. It is the trust that says, "I know this may hurt my partner now, but I trust them to bear with me through it because, in the end, my intention for them is to help them be a better person." You see, we often think of love as a shield for someone, no matter what.

Unfortunately, if we go that route, many times, we shield them from the very thing that God intends to make them grow. We should have the kind of love that will stand with someone in trial and encourage them. Shielding is needed at times, but supporting can often be the better approach to growth.

For example, when Sue and I got married, we each had very complex financial situations alone, let alone trying to combine them. Leading up to our marriage, I had been working diligently to simplify my finances so as to make it easier for us to merge. Sue, on the other hand, had so much going on with open projects that by the time we married, I had become part of that. She just simply could not do much to "simplify" hers. So, when we married, she just took the lead on handling the finances.

For the first couple of years, this was fine as I had a lot on my plate getting a handle on the farm's finances. The farm had grown to a size where there were a lot of transactions and moving parts to track, and the budget was largely made up of a constant infusion from our personal finances to get it off the ground. The venue was largely paid for, and the transactions were far fewer than on the farm. Also, Sue understood the load of business, personal, and corporate inputs and outputs better than I did.

As time went on, this situation changed and evolved to where it is now, which is a place where the farm finances have begun to stabilize and the personal finances have stabilized, and now Sue needs time to market and run the businesses so as the discussion went, we came to the same conclusion that it was time for me to take on the household finances as well as the farm.

Now, if we had just said at the beginning that I was taking the finances, it would not have gone well because of many factors. Sue didn't feel any more comfortable giving them up than I did taking on all of her activity at that time. Now, my teaching from the church when I was a young man said that "the man is the head of the house, and therefore, he must handle the finances, and it needs to be done immediately." Proverbs 31 paints us a very different picture of how things can work in accordance with God's perfect plan for a man and a woman.

Trust needed to happen, a little at first, then to be tried and built upon quickly to bring our two worlds together; all the while, growth continued to happen. When I left Chrysler to work on the farm full-time, she had to trust me to be diligent about working on the farm until it became successful. I needed to trust Sue to have my best interest at heart in how the money would be spent, and she needed to trust me that I was going to not just throw a load of everything on her indefinitely or completely and just check out. This is only one example of where trust is important in a marriage, but finances are a big area.

Trust is much like faith. If we have faith in God, we trust Him to have our best interests at heart. When we go through trials, and we all do, we can be victims and try to find who is to blame. Or we can simply trust that God is watching and waiting for us to grow through them. Scripture tells us that He will never leave us nor forsake us and that He will provide a way of escape should a trial become too much for us to bear.

The question is: Do we believe this? Not do we believe God is real, nor do we believe that he answers our prayers when we get what we asked for, but do we believe that even when we lose a loved one at an early age or when we have to file bankruptcy, or when the sickness just seems to linger on and on, do we believe that God is looking out for our best interest. You see, just like in a good marriage, trust is built through communication and trial. If you never go through a trial, there will be no testing. Without testing, there simply is no need to grow. With no need to grow, growth does not happen.

After my accident, I had a couple of fractures in my shoulder blade that were having some trouble knitting back together. The doctor was trying some different techniques, but the one he wanted to do was not generally paid for by most insurance companies. He had to do some work to get them to buy into it. The technique used was ultrasonic therapy to vibrate the bone near the fracture point, which stimulated growth. The bone had to be tested ever so slightly to make the body realize that growth was needed to heal the fracture. If the testing was too much, too fast, it would have just caused the bone to open up a bigger fracture all over again.

God knows how to test and to what level to test us to stimulate growth without causing more injury. He built us, and He knows how to grow us. Romans 5 says this about the steps in which God grows us:

"And not only so, but we glory in tribulations also: knowing that tribulation worketh patience; and patience, experience; and experience, hope: and hope maketh not ashamed; because the love of God is shed abroad in our hearts by the Holy Ghost which is given unto us."

None of us has ever walked in God's perfect love as we live in this life, save one. That is to say that we are not perfected in this life; there has never been one perfect other than Jesus Christ Himself, who also demonstrated to us what love is. Jesus walked as a man, yet he was God. He brought with Him love, which is correction, longsuffering, and forbearing, having purchased us by His blood, set down at the right hand of the Father to both cheer us on and bring us to the cross where His blood is laid on our behalf that we might be overcomers.

Life goes on through storms and trials, good and bad. It is all part of our Father's plan to help us grow and become strong. If we had never experienced trials, we would not have developed the strength to do more. When a child is shielded too heavily by the parent, it never develops the strength to stand on its own. When the trials come in too strong, if we do not shield our children before they are ready, they will drown or be burned up. How much more does our heavenly Father understand this than we do, and how much more does He love us than we can love others?

Overcoming is learning to trust. When our trust in God grows so do the trials. This is not to say He will leave us or abandon us, it is to say that He understands what we can handle. To be an overcomer is not about our strength it is rather a statement of how much we have learned to rely on His ever-saving grace and mercy.

I have shared many of my life's trials; they are unique, but they are also common. Everyone gets their own share of trials in life; Jesus promised us that in this life, we will have suffering. It's not what happens to you that counts; rather, it is how you deal with what you are dealt. When we focus on ourselves and all of the wrongs that have happened to us, we get stuck. We need to focus on God instead and understand that He has the capability to change anything on a dime. But the other part is that when we focus on this life alone, we will miss what God has prepared for us in eternity. We are eternal beings. How we spend that eternity depends on how we relate to our creator while we are here in this life. We cannot be perfect or good enough to receive anything but judgment. What we can receive by trusting in God and overcoming what is in this world is an eternity with God, ruling and reigning with Him.

When we walk an overcoming walk, we will walk in the calling that God has called us to. I have heard many, many times, "How do we know when God has called us to do something?" I would say if you are following God, then you should do the thing that is in your heart. Do the thing He has given you talent and love for. If you do this, then you are walking in the thing He has called you to. God equips those who follow Him with the tools they need to do the thing He calls them to. Psalms says this: "Delight thyself in the Lord, and He will give you the desires of your heart." If He puts a desire in your heart, this is your calling.

Yes, there will be challenges to overcome. There will be opposition to you being successful, make no mistake. Satan is real, and he seeks to destroy. But greater is He that is in you that He that is in the world. Trust in the Lord and He will bring it to past. When we dream about something, when we have a God-given desire to do a thing, He will equip us to perform it.

As I have been writing thus far, I have been sharing with you the history of my life experiences and how God has taught me to lean on Him and walk with Him daily.

This morning, 7 January 2025, I was awoken at 5:30 am with a desire in my heart that seemed quite odd to me indeed. I suddenly felt the need to learn to play the clarinet. As if from completely out of the blue. As I prayed about this, I said to God, "But you have placed this book on my heart also; I have hit a dead spot in writing and no desire to finish it." As I prayed about it, it seemed to come to me to change the direction of the book from a historical account and lessons learned to a current account of my daily walk in a diary fashion and to share with my reader my life and how God is directing. So, from this point forward, I will be walking with you through my current situation.

As such, I will share with you this strange, seemingly God-sent desire to learn to play the clarinet out of the blue. As a young child, I always loved music, and my mom saw this. I loved to listen to music and imagine many things while listening.

When I was in the 5th grade, I wanted to join the band at school. Now, being the youngest of 10 children, and with many of my older sisters being in a band already and my parents not being rich, I was told I could learn to play the clarinet, which was an instrument my older sister had already so there would be no cost of buying another instrument for my parents, and we could find out just how strong my desire was. Well, in the 5th grade back then, for a boy to play the clarinet was not very acceptable as a "boyish" thing to do. I wanted to play the cornet or trumpet. However, I wanted to learn to be musical, so I agreed to play the clarinet. I tried it for a while, but the stigma of being a boy playing clarinet impeded my learning, and I ended up dropping out.

Years later, I still had that desire to play something and be musical. I loved singing in church and always did my best to sing out loud. I guess I had skilled hands, or at least my mom thought so, so for my 15th birthday, my mom bought me a guitar. I loved it! I played and played and taught myself well enough to begin playing at church. In time, I would become a music leader at church, playing my guitar. Later, I led music at several churches. I just seemed to gravitate there. I always love to sing loudly to the Lord.

These days, I have once again been led back to a role where I am once again leading at church on occasion. Sue and I attend Whiteford Wesleyan church, and I find great joy in leading the congregation in worship from time to time. The pastors there both play the piano, and we have an organ player. From time to time, members of the congregation have played instruments, and when I lead, I still use the same guitar my mom bought me. I have expressed to the new young pastor my desire to see more instruments being played in the worship. And we have discussed ways to promote interest for people to do so.

Now, Sue's youngest boy plays the trumpet and he has been part of many very impressive music shows. We have often traveled to see him play and we have enjoyed concerts at the college where he has played, I think now that with the combination of things in my life coming to a stable place once again, it would be a perfect time to expand my abilities to give the good Lord thanks for all that He has done in my life.

When I awoke this morning with the thought of learning to play the clarinet specifically, it seemed a very strange thought to me. However, now that I have thought about it and taken the time to write it down, I realize it might not be so strange after all. In His Word, God tells us to praise him on the psaltery and the harp and on all manner of instruments. We are created to praise Him. And with as much talent as we are given to do so, we ought to have the utmost desire to praise Him as He has given us life. He has redeemed us from sin and bought us at a high price. We ought to have a burning desire in us to worship and praise Him. This morning, as I write this, I am listening to Mozart's Concerto in A major for clarinet, which was beautifully performed by Sharon Kam.

Now, I know what you may be thinking. This is a whimsical desire, and maybe I'll spend some money on a clarinet and give it a try, but it will fade away. Well, I would be lying if I told you that every time, I set out to do something, I see it through. Take flying, for example. I started flight lessons and got to the point where I was within a few flight hours of getting a private pilot's license. The reason for starting had passed, and the expense of flying had become too much of a burden to continue. Also, my wife had no desire to get into a small plane, so it was never going to be something I would use. But God had used that time for His purpose of answering my prayer to find a career in engineering. Had I not taken those lessons, I would not have met Troy, who used his influence at Chrysler to help me get into the role. A role he held and left just as I was coming in. I don't know why I woke up at 5:30 this morning thinking I should learn to play the clarinet, but if God has planted that in me, then surely, He will use it for His purposes for me, and it may be that He just wants to hear another clarinet in the orchestra in eternity. I will keep you tuned in to see how this goes.

From this point forward in the book, I will write the things about the day that I feel God has laid upon my heart to write. As 2025 gets underway, many things will happen both in the world and at home. While the world seems to continue to descend into complete turmoil and the price of living seems to be getting out of sight, for Sue and I, God has brought us to a place of ever-increasing stability and growth. The farm is doing well, and our two worlds are coming together nicely. There were a lot of things to sort through: mental and emotional baggage, mountains of belongings of two households merging, changing career paths, financial upheaval, and two families of children who are still learning the throes of adulthood. God has blessed us richly to be able to handle so many changes with grace and continue moving forward with stride while giving grace unto others.

Today is a day of thanksgiving for all that God has done. For He has richly blessed me and restored me from a low place. He has set me in a place of rejoicing even for all that He has done. It is winter, and the birds have been quiet. The flowers are shut up in the ground as if it was a grave. The trees are bare, and the air is cold. Yet the sun is shining today, and there is reason to hope. For God has set all these things to be according to His time. While all is quiet, He has seen fit to promote me. There are cattle in the stalls waiting to give birth and young pigs in the stall with their sow. The sheep are in the barn breeding for spring deliveries, and there is promise of good things to come. The venue has been bustling, and there is a wedding to celebrate this Saturday. Sue remains busy with work, but she is working towards exiting Vitamix. The boiler is now up and running on the farm, and the house is staying warm. We have been in work and toil over many things, but God has brought blessings to our work. We serve a great God, a good, good Father. Though the world may be in ruin and though the sky may be dark, we have reason to hope. God has promised to keep us till all these things are fulfilled, and He returns to rule and reign here among us. The Lord is great and greatly to be praised.

We had a bull calf born at the end of November, and we named him Moses. He is red like his mother and doing very well out on the cold mornings. He is always full of joy and running about. When I look at him, I see things the way they should be. He doesn't complain about the cold; he does not lay around mopping because he wants to play, and it is muddy. He simply goes out and runs and plays and enjoys life. He is healthy and has much to be thankful for, though I do not think cattle think about such things. Yet he gives glory to God, as all of creation should. We are fearfully and wonderfully made and have been given life again after sin, for Jesus has come! He has paid the price so that we might have life and life more abundantly.

I plan to get out in the cold myself today and cut some wood for the wood burner. We will continue to burn wood and use it as the primary heating source for the house, even though the boiler is running now. Why, you might ask. Well, to keep the bill down for one, and for another reason, it gives me work to do, and it's so enjoyable to sit by the warm fire on these cold days. I have spent many hours in prayer and reflection, sitting in front of the wood burner with a hot cup of delicious coffee in hand. It has become a place of peace and quiet for me, something everyone should have in their life. The Lord said in His Word to be still and know that He is God. To wait on the Lord is wisdom. We cannot, by all of our work, accomplish more than God does for us in our resting. Overcoming is an act of faith and trust, not work. The Word does not say they overcame him by their works. It says they overcame him by the blood of the Lamb and the Word of their testimony. The Word of our testimony should be Jesus Christ and what He has done for us, especially and personally. Well, it is after ten o'clock now, and I need to get to work on some wood cutting.

It is 13 January, and I have completed my first self-lesson on the clarinet. Sue and I went to Claire's house last evening and picked it up. Claire is Sue's middle child, and she played the clarinet in high school. She apparently played very well and earned the honors of 1st chair every year. She had many of her old lesson sheets, and she gave them to me also.

Now, at my age, it will likely be a daunting task to self-teach an instrument, let alone be in shape enough to do it. I started studying to learn to read music as well as exercising to strengthen my lung muscles. Teaching my mouth to shape the mouthpiece and produce clear notes is the next step in the exercises at this point. Teaching my brain to see notes and translate them to my fingers. Teaching my patients to bear with all my mistakes and shortcomings is, for me, perhaps the biggest lesson I will learn from it all. God has brought me to a very good place indeed to be able to afford the time and still have the desire and wherewithal to learn an instrument at 53 is no small thing. I think we often fail to appreciate things because we don't understand what is required to have or achieve them. Desire, drive, and discipline are all things that God has given us. Desire drives us to a thing, a talent, or a relationship. Drive is the compelling force that pushes us to strive to acquire, achieve, and maintain what we have. Discipline, either internal or external, is what steers us and pushes us through hardships along the way.

Psalms 37:4 says, "Delight thyself also in the Lord: and he shall give thee the desires of thine heart." When you delight in the Lord, He will plant a thing in you that will draw you to the place where you can use the talents He has put in you and help you develop the skills needed to perform those desires well. When Solomon asked God for wisdom, God not only gave him wisdom, but He also added to it wealth. Wisdom to rule the people well and wealth to honor God with a temple where the people could come to meet with God and bring the sacrifices that were commanded of them by God. God can and will equip you to do things that are pleasing to you when you ask of Him because you love Him. James 4:2-3 says, "Ye lust, and have not: ye kill, and desire to have, and cannot obtain: ye fight and war, yet ye have not, because ye ask not. Ye ask, and receive not, because ye ask amiss, that ye may consume it upon your lusts." So then, when you ask, ask out of a desire to be pleasing unto God and not for yourself.

To be an overcomer, our testimony must be that we love him, who has created us and loved us first, so that he gave Himself so that we might be saved from our sin.

I hope that in learning to play the clarinet, God can use that in some way to further His kingdom as I recall the feeling I had when the desire to leave Chrysler and start a farm and compare that now to the desire to learn to play the clarinet, the two are very similar inside of me. Now, when I look back on all that has happened and is happening since the onset of starting the farm, I see God's hand at work in me and through me. Not only for my own good but also for the good of so many I have been in contact with because of the farm. Trials have come, and losses have occurred, yet God has always been faithful to carry not just me but now Sue and me through them and make us stronger because of them.

It is very cold today and the current cold front looks like it will be with us for a while. When I say cold, we are in the single digits at night and do not climb out of the teens in the day. It has us staying housebound for sure. And with that, there is plenty of time for learning and practicing a new skill, such as playing the clarinet. I also will be leading music at church on Sunday so there is work to be done to prepare for that.

It is 14th February, and the cold winter has once again reared its head. We expect to see temps near and below zero in the week ahead, and it seems as though I may have time to catch up on a bit of writing.

Things have gotten busy again and the clarinet playing took a back seat to the activities of running a farm/ranch, as it seems writing has as well.

We have had 4 calves born so far this winter and they are all healthy. The first one however was rather touch and go for a while. Alex was born on a very cold morning in January, and when I got to him, he was nearly gone. He was so cold he could barely move. Hypothermia had set in and it required intensive care to bring him back around.

After a night in the house next to the wood burner, however, he seemed to take off just fine. Now he is back with his mother, and they are with the herd. He is wearing a coat for the next week, however, as it will be blistering cold. The other three calves, two heifers, and another bull are doing well. The heifers are white like their mothers, and the two bulls are black. The herd is all doing well, and we expect two more to arrive in March.

When the cold settled in back in January, I turned on the hot water to the barns. Apparently, the heat was too much for the underground line, and it ruptured.

So, I have been hauling water to the barns and using buckets to get everyone watered. It is a laborious, cold task and consumes a great deal of time. But thank God for the water hauler because, without it, I wouldn't have been able to get the job done. The chorus goes on daily, and the winter winds on. There is a blanket of snow on the ground today, and the sun is shining brightly, although it is difficult to capture any heat from its rays. There is never too much downtime here, though, because if you stop, the world just seems to spin even faster. We are planning for spring and the next season of growth.

Baby chicks arrived yesterday, fifty egg layers of various breeds. With the increasing war on our food supply in this country, many people are turning from grocery stores to buying directly from a farmer. The bird flu has taken a toll on egg production as well as poultry meat. Prices are high if you can find eggs in the store at all. Many people are trying to get chickens of their own now, and they are looking to their local farm to do it. So, we are ramping up our poultry program as fast as we can to help in this war. Cattle have also been affected, though not to the same degree yet.

Our pigs are doing well. We sold 5 of the 9 from our first litter, born to Lucy back in November; the other four are slated for processing for pork sales. The sheep are well-behaved sheep, just waiting to get out of the barn in the spring to have their baby lambs.

Plans go on, and time passes. Relationships grow and die, and life goes on. As we get older, troubles go on, but we know that through God's good graces and mercy, we can and will overcome. We get news from the kids from time to time about things they are working on, though we do not see them as often as we would like. It is enough to know that they are doing well these days. Sue and I have been together for nearly 3 years, and our relationship is a three-year marriage, I suppose.

The daily tasks of washing dishes and laundry, tending the wood stove, and cleaning the house are shared tasks with an acceptance that sometimes they just go undone, and that's okay. We both work from home, so we are here all day together, and that, for me, is the way it should be.

This world has torn the family unit so far apart now, with financial struggles and two or more jobs or careers in a home that pulls a husband and wife apart, and for what? So that we might obtain material things that do us little good. The government is taxing people into poverty in the name of helping those in poverty. It is one big evil merry-go-round where the rulers become richer and the ruled become subjugated.

This once-free country has become Babylon, Rome, England, and every other system that men have ever created. To survive in such a place, one must learn to be happy with little and understand that the kingdom of God is not here on this earth in its entirety at this point. We have a portion of the kingdom in that we have salvation, but we see another ruler here, an evil one.

That is to say, we see the work of the devil everywhere and we must work, we must fight for that which God has given us. When God told the Israelites that the promised land was theirs, He did not remove all the giants from it.

When He told Neihamiah to build a wall, He did not remove all of the opposition. Even when He sent His own son, He did not remove all of those opposed to the kingdom. It is within His power to do these things, so why does He leave it up to us to fight? We fight for what God has given us to show our faith. We fight because we believe in what God is doing.

One of the worst things that you can do to a man is to take away his sense of purpose. To remove the very reason for his being. If we have nothing to work for, if we have nothing to fight for, what then is the reason? We were created to bring pleasure to God, the Creator of all things. If He created us to work, to have a purpose, to be the caretakers of His creation, how then do we believe a lie that tells us idle time is good? Yet we are told to take time to rest, to save for retirement, and to live a life of luxury, which is the goal. Rest is good for a season, but when it becomes the goal, our sense of purpose quickly fades, and we become lazy. Laziness and idle hands accomplish nothing and are good for nothing.

We hear so much these days about mental health issues, and so many people are on all different kinds of medications, which in most cases are nothing less than tranquilizers; the question is, why? Why are we seeing such an epidemic in mental health? There are many reasons, I suppose, but a couple stands out in my mind. One is the rejection of God and His law for living. Two is poor physical health; when the body is lacking, the mind is not fed and cannot function properly. Third is a lack of purpose, belonging, and general social interactions.

All of these problems are easily solved by understanding the first one and executing it in our daily walk. When we read God's word, He gives us a template of what and what not to do to keep ourselves healthy. A good drive for life is essential to our well-being. We must set forth to do whatever it is that God has laid upon our hearts to do.

Paul says in his writing to set aside every weight that so easily besets us and to run a race. The cares of this life are not ours to carry. Jesus died so that we may set upon Him those cares and run. When we carry the past, we hinder ourselves from the now. Jesus said that in this life you will have suffering, but then He also said, but be of good cheer because I have overcome this world that you may have life and life more abundantly.

When I had the accident with the tree, at first, I was scared. Scared because I didn't know what I would become. Would I be able to recover? Would I be able to work? Would I have a job to return to? In the months that followed the accident, I spent many hours in prayer. The nights were long, sleeping alone on the couch downstairs because I could not get up to move around, much less climb the stairs to go to bed with my wife. I had to trust God. I had to! If He had spared my life, He must still have a purpose for me. So, with that in mind, I began to push. I pushed through the pain, through the discouragement, through the judgment, and into God and His mighty arms. There were many nights I lay there on the couch, and I could almost feel the devil himself whisper in my ear,

"You're going to die." Fear had no place in my walk at that point. There was only God and His promises to me.

When Kris died, I didn't know which way life would turn. I was afraid of doing life alone. I prayed and asked God to send me another wife. He asked me why I needed a wife. I told Him I could not do this alone. He said you're not alone; I am with you. I said I don't want to do this alone. He said I will send you a helper. A woman who will stand by you and make you a better man. And Sue came to me. Together, Sue and I have overcome so much by standing on God's Word and promises.

There is no room for fear. There is no time for fear. There is no room for self-pity, nor is there time for it. God has not given us a spirit of fear but a sound mind. Nothing in this life will come easy, nor should it. For if it comes easy, there is no appreciation for it, and there is no thankfulness. When I look at how people exist these days, I see helplessness. Most people have become completely dependent on governments, corporations, and technologies in order to meet their daily needs. For many, even many Christians, God is nowhere in the equation for how one is provided for. When we lose our dependence on God, we lose the purpose for which we were created. We are to be caretakers of this world; God provided all that was needed for Adam and Eve, and all they needed to do was take care of what He provided.

Now, most depend on the three things I mentioned to provide, and if they go to church on Sunday, it is to be involved in some sort of social group or to be entertained with a feel-good message. Freedom from oppression requires us to have the ability to take care of ourselves in our basic needs of food, water, shelter, and the like. Yes, God provides these things, but we must work to own them and use them for our own good. It is our purpose to be caretakers and to give God glory in the process. God created us with free will, but freedom can only exist when work is done to meet our basic needs. The Word says if a man doesn't work, he does not eat.

The Word also says that Satan is very crafty and subtle, and he uses men to lay traps for other men. One could argue that technology is perhaps the greatest evil that has ever come to mankind. It has made us lazy. It has also caused our population to grow at an unsustainable rate. Governments have used it to control the masses of people. Corporations have used it to become rich and powerful, add further control. We are slaves to it. I walk out among my livestock, and I see how they are dependent upon me to feed them and care for them, yet they are being raised for food. The cows have come to like the shelter of the barn, and the pigs could not survive the cold of winter without it. There are inherent issues with livestock being held in close proximity for long periods of time. Diseases and weakness develop.

To combat this, most farmers and ranchers turn to vaccines and medicines, which further weaken the animals and spread to those who consume them. We have been told a great lie. Something has to change. Something, maybe everything will change.

As we work our way through February, the snow continues to come down today. The world is white and cold. The cows stay in the barn most of the day, looking out the doors, waiting for the change of spring to come, waiting to see green grass again and feel the warm summer sun. The smells of flowers and fresh-cut fields. We, too, wait for spring. We wait for Jesus to return and set things right again. To renew the land, to bring back righteousness and holiness. As I mentioned, Sue and I are planning many new things to do on the farm in the spring, making improvements and restoring what is already here. The act of building something is, in some form, an apprenticeship, I think, for what is to come. We are created in God's image, and we were intended to do so much more than what we know. We are to one day rule and reign with Him.

There is much to learn, and while we cannot learn it all here, we must begin, for life eternal begins now. Overcoming is the beginning of ruling and reigning; it is a foundation for it.

Vision

Perhaps the hardest thing we can ever seek to find is our own true nature. Often, we become so burdened with life activities, outside influences, and cultural norms that we allow to shape us that we lose the person who God created us to be. We are each created to be unique; our qualities, likes and dislikes, and how we react to things are all unique. I have been doing some self-reflection lately. I am now far enough removed by time from events that were significant in shaping who I am now to look back and see my own reactions to them.

I am realizing that for many years, the quiet, gentle boy I was as a youngster had gotten buried so that I could deal with life as a young man with a family, then an older man in charge of a large group of people, an empty nester, a widower, a second-time newlywed, and a business owner.

As I grew through these roles in life, that small, gentle boy became a man who sometimes lost that gentleness. Now that I am settled once again into marriage, my children are grown and have their own children, and my new wife is often busy with her own things, I have time to reflect and ask myself: what kind of man do I want to be? You have become an overcomer when you reach a place where you can decide this for yourself rather than thinking about what others think, worrying about life's demands, or simply being too busy keeping up. One who can have a testimony of your own. The word of your testimony is the overcoming.

Over the last several years, God has afforded me several opportunities to reflect on where I have been and where I am going. Mostly, these times have come through tragedy. But each time, I find myself going through them with more grace and dignity, knowing that my Father in heaven works on things to my good and that there is no trial that will befall me that He has not already given me the strength to handle.

When we look at the great men of the Bible, we see times when they did not handle things well and times when they did. When they obeyed God, victories were handed to them by God. When they thought of doing things their own way, they struggled and sometimes paid a very high price for their lack of faith or obedience. It is extremely important for you to look back on your own life and see when you have obeyed God and when you have not. This will help you shape the kind of person you want to be moving forward.

Sometimes, obedience requires boldness and courage, and other times, it requires humbleness and meekness. It is important to look back and see when you reacted correctly so that you can tune your listening skills to match those moments.

Course Planning and Adjustments

There have been times when I felt God said very plainly to do something or to make a course change, but when I did what I thought He was asking me, it all went bad, or at least it seemed to. Opposition will usually come as soon as you step into what God is asking you to do. This is not the time to second-guess. Jesus said that a man who has set out to plow a field, looking back, is not fit for the kingdom of God. If you have ever tried to plow a field, you know there is great opposition to it.

The land will fight you, the horse must be driven to do the work, and the heat of the day will wear you out. Very few decisions, if any, come with guarantees of success. But if you waver in a decision made, then it is almost certain that success will not be achieved.

It did not take long for Sue and I to make the decision to get married. It seems that God has brought us together through many circumstances and events in life at such a time that we would be ready to do the thing that we are doing now. We are drawing on every bit of our life experiences, training, and education to pull together the launching of two businesses, a marriage and a family, all simultaneously. There are some decisions that we have made that were once set in stone. Getting married, for example, has never been questioned.

Once we decided on this, we knew it didn't need any further discussion. You don't second-guess that once those vows are said. Sadly, this is not the case for many people. Marriage is entered into with the idea that as long as I keep feeling the same way I do now, I will keep my vows. This leads to infidelity of all kinds. There are times when our feelings betray us, and we need to ignore them and stay the course.

Another reason commitments often fail is that we don't fully understand what we are committing to and did not do our due diligence to find out beforehand. Jesus also speaks to this when he says that a man setting out to build a house who has not weighed the cost and begins it but is unable to finish it because he runs out of money or materials is laughed at as a fool. We owe ourselves and others to take the time to understand commitments before entering them so that we know whether or not we will be able to complete them.

It does no one any good to tell them you can do something for them if you, in fact, cannot, just make them feel better for a time, because, in the end, you both pay the price when the thing is not done. Being a man or woman of your word is a priceless and timeless commodity that is in very short supply these days, sad as it is.

Well, with the costs weighed, the decision made, and the level of commitment at all in status, there's no looking back. It's straight on to success, right? Well, not so fast. Have you considered the impact on those around you of what you are going to engage in? What do your shareholders think? Is your spouse on board? How will it impact your children?

These are the extended costs that may not be pivotal to the success of a new venture, but certainly can help or hinder progress if not considered. The buy-in of a spouse is of utmost importance, and while we may not always agree, we need to come to a consensus so that when trouble comes along, and it will, the decision to move forward is a joint one. Otherwise, there will be division and inevitable failure.

As the farm grew and the learning curve became steep, Sue and I asked ourselves many times, "What are we doing?" But I think we both understood well that we were doing what God put us here to do. There have been many trials, and many times, we did not feel adequate for the job. We had to trust God and know that He knew what He was doing. Whenever we found ourselves in a tight spot, He always seemed to send someone to help. Whether it was cattle on the loose running down the road or a breakdown on the side of the highway trying to haul farm equipment back to the house, He always made a way. Now, as we look deeper into what is happening to our food supply and the American farm, I think we understand more and more every day why we are doing what we are doing. The purpose is important to our well-being. We must have a purpose in our lives to remain engaged and productive. Without it, depression sets in, and many become disengaged altogether in life. God intended us to take care of this earth and to have dominion over it. We have done a poor job of that.

Power is a terrible motivator and many terrible things have come from the search for it and the desire to have it. Technology has also brought terrible consequences to our world, but when the two of them are coupled together, we witness the worst of man.

We must abandon our quest for power to overcome the enemy and understand that while technology can make our lives easier, God intended us to work and manage this world. Sue and I have begun to drive our farm back to the old ways of doing things, with a few exceptions. We run a diverse livestock farm, and we are seeking to manage our land in a way that will improve it, not just to profit from it. When Adam and Eve sinned, a curse followed, and man has fought that curse ever since. We battle weeds, thistles, and thorns to grow crops; we battle diseases and the like to raise livestock. This is the curse, but when we seek to overcome that curse with technologies such as chemicals and larger equipment, we actually do more harm than good. God has a way to block these things, and that is to give a portion of all that we do back to him. The Bible says that when we give our tithe, God will rebuke the devourer for us, and we will see more increase than what we ever give Him.

As we understand farming, we see the abuses that this world has taken in the name of progress. Now, if we can turn some of that back, even just in our own little corner, we will do all we can. As we do, we are working to help others do the same. Sharing the gospel is not just preaching. It is living it. Living out what God has commanded us to do in the most basic sense is to take care of the land and animals and manage them in a way that will cause them to flourish and provide for us.

Quality of Life

Success can be defined in so many different ways, and I suppose we each have our own unique definition for it. So, I guess one could say that there are as many definitions of success as there are people who seek it. One thing is clear, however: the term "quality of life" cannot be defined in monetary terms alone. As we grow and mature, most begin to understand this.

For some, quality of life is about family at all costs; for others, it is about how big the bank account is or how many assets are accumulated. Still, others like to have time to themselves to travel or experience all this life has to offer. For some, however, we understand that this life is short at best and that the real success is laying up treasures in the hereafter. We do, all of us, have a life to live in the here and now, though, and the way we live that life can be not only rewarding now but also for eternity.

Scripture says that all things should be done in moderation. This is to say that if we allow any one dynamic of life to dominate over all else, we miss the true quality of life. Too much focus on money for example can ruin our relationships and our health. Too much attention to our physical health can become damaging to our spiritual health and our financial health.

So, how do we find a balance in all things? God's Word gives us a wealth of examples and prescriptions for this. We would do well to understand first God's reason for creating us and, secondly, God's intent for how we are to fulfill His direction for our lives. Each of us is given talents, which, when best used, give glory to our creator who so richly bestowed them upon us. In addition to talents, we have desires, things we like, and things we dislike. One must look deep into God's intentions to gain an understanding of His will for us and the particular talents and desires He has given us.

Let's take a look into some of the earliest accounts of what happens when we don't look closely to understand, one what God is asking, and two how our gifts can be used to facilitate that.

In King James' version of Genesis 3:21, we see that God showed man exactly what was required for the covering of sins. The verse says this:

"Unto Adam also and to his wife did the Lord God make coats of skins and clothed them."

Now, one could argue that God "created" coats of skin for them, but that's not what it says. It says He made them. Which is to say an animal had to be sacrificed and blood given. Back up to verse 17 of chapter 2, you'll see that the punishment for eating the tree of the knowledge of good and evil was death. But it was not only the death of Adam and Eve; it was the death of all that was created on Earth. God said that on the day they ate of the tree, they would die. The serpent who lied to Eve understood that a day with the Lord is not the same as a day in our life; therefore, he could tell Eve that she would not die on that day and not even be telling a lie.

However, Adam and Eve did, in fact, die on the day that they ate of the tree because Scripture tells us that with God, a day is a thousand years and a thousand years as a day. Neither Adam nor Eve nor anyone after them ever lived to be a thousand years old. Death was a certain punishment for sin, and it infected all of creation. However, to be free from one's own death, the death of another in that person's stead would become payment for that sin. In the Old Testament, we see that God allowed for the death of animals to be a covering of sin. But this was no more than a foreshadowing of His promise yet to come, but more on that later.

For now, let's get back to the understanding that Cain should have been aware of when he offered his own sacrifice for sin.

You see, when God gave an example to Adam and Eve of the animal sacrifice, it became known to them that this was His plan, at least for their time to deal with their sin. This was, in no doubt, shared with their sons as they grew, and Cain and Abel understood that they must offer their own sacrifices. The acceptable sacrifice made well known to them was why Cain offered the fruit of ground rather than an animal. Well, Scripture tells us that Cain was a tiller of the ground and a farmer. At the same time, Abel was a keeper of the sheep and a herdsman.

So, let's dive into Cain's mind for a minute. If I till the ground, and my God-given talent is for that, and I like doing it, then God should accept an offering of what I do as a use of the talent He gave me, right? This is the subtlety of Satan.

Furthermore, when Cain saw that God was not pleased with his thought to replace the prescribed sacrifice of blood with something else, Cain had a chance to go and trade with Abel for a sheep and sacrifice that. But he chose another path. A path of sin. Cain became upset that Abel had pleased God and he did not.

Once he became hurt, instead of working to fix the problem, he made things worse by lashing out at the one who had done it right, as if that would somehow right his wrong. So why was it difficult for Cain to get it right? Pride, shame, guilt, or maybe he just wasn't that smart. There are many lessons to be learned here. But the one I want to take away now is the fact that if Cain had just taken the time to examine what the sacrifice needed to be and why it needed to be what it was, then maybe he would have been able to trade some corn and onions to Abel for a sheep and offered the correct sacrifice.

To overcome the wiles of the devil, we must understand what God has asked and follow it even if we don't understand the way for now. God's prescription for our lives does not necessarily reflect our talents, skills, likes, and dislikes. That doesn't mean that there is something wrong with us. It simply means we must learn how to apply those things in a way that can get us to the prescribed method of living.

The Great Commission

Much like Cain, I was not given the calling to be a preacher, but then again, most of us are not. However, we are still all given the commandment to "go and make disciples and to deliver the gospel into all the world." For each of us, the way in which we do this will look different, of course. I was given the talent to be able to look into complex systems and understand how they work. I applied this to being a mechanic first of all and then to becoming a process engineer.

Now, I'm building a business and running a livestock farm and ranch. So, the question I ask myself is: how do I do what Cain *should* have done—learn to use my talents in a way that fulfills God's specific command to go forth and multiply His Kingdom? One way might be to teach others how to become farmers or engineers, equipping them with the skills to earn a living and live with purpose.

Certainly, this would be "good work," right? But does it fulfill the commandment to build the Kingdom? Jesus said that many will stand before the Lord on the day of judgment and say, "Lord, we have cast out devils in your name and have done many great works," to which He will answer, "Depart from me ye workers of inquiry I never knew you." What is He saying? It's simply this: if we do not do the things that He has given us to do as our primary objective, all the works we do in His name will be counted as ashes. Did he command His disciples to cast out demons or even feed the poor? Well, these are good things to do, but if they are not coupled with His primary commandment to spread the good news, they are useless in themselves.

As Sue and I build our businesses, the farm/ranch, and the wedding venue, we strive to keep in mind that these are merely tools to get us into a position to spread the Good News to a lost world. The people that we come in contact with need to hear and see Christians living a Christian life. Setting examples of how to be good stewards in keeping the world that God has laid in our trust to keep and have dominion over. But even more importantly than that, it's demonstrating that we need a savior and that God has provided one for us in Jesus Christ.

From the beginning, Satan has been working to thwart God's plan for man. When he deceived Eve into sin, however, he had only set in motion God's plan from the foundations of this world. That was that Jesus would come and live among us and die as a man, crucified and set as a sacrifice to redeem us from a bad choice to take a step in the wrong direction of free will. We were created with free will, and God has never revoked it from us. In fact, He has time and again set in place a means for us to return to Him after making a wrong decision. He waits for each of us to decide; the Holy Spirit calls to us and beckons us to come to Him.

As Christians, we are to join in this call to the lost to woo them to the cross, where Jesus paid the price of blood for sin. We should be living such a life as to not only be an example but an attraction for people to want to know Jesus.

Failure and Success as Attractions

People like to be around successful people. Whether learning from them, gathering energy from them, or just admiring them, we like to be around those doing well. Success can be measured in many ways; financial stability, health, relationships, and popularity can all be measurements of success. Oddly enough, failure can also attract people.

When people see someone fall into failure, they often want to help in some way. But witnessing a person rise from failure to success—that's the kind of story that resonates deeply. It's the story many of us hope to live ourselves. Everyone experiences failure at some point, and when someone finds a way to overcome it, others naturally want to understand how. They hope to apply those lessons to their own lives and become the kind of success story that inspires and uplifts others.

Numerous books have been written about the secret to success, and most of these books focus on one type of success only. Money is perhaps the most sought-after, but relationship success is also a very popular bookseller. There are few who talk about the recipe for complete success across the board. And there are none that do it with the authority that is contained within the Word of God. When we demonstrate the application of the Word to our lives, we will demonstrate success at all levels. Does this mean we will be wealthy, healthy, happy, and wise? Well, not in terms of how this world measures those things, but it most certainly does. Eternal wealth should be the focus of our hearts and minds, however, if we learn to apply the principles in God's Word to this life, I think that in most cases we will find that money becomes a "non-issue" for us. Being rich is not on God's agenda for every one of us. He calls each of us to walk in a different lane in life so that His light might shine through us to all that dwell on this earth.

If God made every Christian rich, would the poor see a demonstration of His goodness to them? If God healed every physical ailment that may befall, how would so many in the hospitals be ministered to? Even the poor in spirit have a place in God's Kingdom when they look to Him for their source. The Scripture says that if any man lacks wisdom, he should ask the Father, who gives so liberally.

Shortly after Sue and I got married, we both began to hear the Holy Spirit saying to us, "We would have need of nothing." Now, we didn't really know what that meant at first, but as time has gone on, we have seen Him meeting our needs in ways we never could have imagined. Rarely does God bless people in terms of hard cash. God's economy is not measured in monetary terms. He meets all of our needs, physical, emotional, spiritual, etc., in ways that only He can do.

When the Israelites left Egypt, they really didn't even understand what their needs would be. They didn't know where they were going. They had no idea how long it would take to get there or what difficulties lay in wait along the way. But as they traveled and situations arose God meant their needs and not once was it done with money or material things.

God could have provided boats to cross the sea, but He didn't. Instead, He changed the sea. He could have multiplied the cattle that they took from Egypt to feed them all meat. Instead, He gave them manna from the sky. When they complained about the manna, He sent the quail for meat. God provides in sorts of ways, usually in ways we don't anticipate. He didn't heal every person of physical disease or ailments; for some, He gave grace and spiritual growth to be able to find happiness in their situation.

Overcoming is learning to accept what God gives us as all that we need. In doing so, we will find that we will have need of nothing because He is the great provider. When we come to a place we can show success even through our failures. Paul said that he took great comfort in his infirmities, for he knew that by them, God was working out a more perfect Paul. Sometimes, that thing we think is our greatest hindrance is the very thing that God is using to grow us, and we should learn to embrace it as a means to run to Jesus for help.

Law of Attraction

While successes and failures can act as attractants, there is another quality about people that can make them attractive without even looking into their success or failure. When we see someone completely and totally sold out of the thing they do, they somehow become attractive. Take, for example, the symbol of the American Cowboy, you know, the romantic one that rides away into the sunset. It doesn't truly matter whether he got the girl or not. When the movie is over, we don't care whether he was able to keep the ranch; we care about whether he lived on to be a cowboy and to keep doing the thing that he loves.

There is something about watching a person do the thing they truly love. They do it not for power, money, or notoriety; they simply do it because it's what they love. A musician who performs in a symphony often does not get any praise for their individual performance; they do it because they love playing their instrument.

When we live a Christian life because we love Jesus and we love serving Him, people see it and want it. Often, they don't even know what "it" is, but they see something, a quality of life, that they want to feel. People will get close to you and watch to see if they can understand it. This kind of testimony cannot be put into words. It must be demonstrated.

The cowboy cannot tell you enough about what he does to make you understand why he loves doing it. And being a cowboy isn't for everyone. Jesus said that all would come to repentance, but sadly, even the Kingdom of God is not for everyone; he said as many as do receive me to Him. He will give the power to become the sons of God. To be a cowboy, you have to want it; you have to fight for it. It does not come easy, nor does the hard stuff ever go away. There are times when you have to bury a favorite dog or horse.

There are times when a newborn calf does not make it. The everyday mundane task can mount up and become overwhelming. But then there are the sunsets. There are days when the new calves are running and playing in the warm summer sun. The birds singing in the meadow and the fresh smell of rain as it falls on a spring morning. God's creation has no bounds of wonder and amazement for those who take the time to look. And to serve the Creator of it all cannot be described by all the words known to man.

Every relationship is as unique as the person holding it. When that relationship is bounded by love, it is as attractive as the song of the entire creation singing all together in one unified symphony.

2025

It is now March, and nature has started to turn her focus to spring. The air is getting warmer, and the frost is beginning to leave the ground. With new baby chicks arriving and the incubator full of eggs set to hatch, we are anticipating a very busy springtime.

The cows are continuing to deliver their calves, and Lucy and Tank are working on the next batch of little piggies. Lavern and Sherlyn have both been in with Lenny all winter, and we expect lambs to be delivered in May. With all of this going on, Sue and I have decided to open a storefront at the farm to bring in more products and meet more of what people are looking for from an area farm market.

The Bedford Press, an area newspaper, just published a full feature article on the farm last week and it seems we have become all the buzz around the community for our products and our impact on the community. We are working to improve to curb appeal of the farm with landscaping and new siding on the barns this year. A greenhouse and pumpkin patch are in the work plans and they are sure to continue to attract more folks to the farm.

While we hope all of these things will continue to increase revenue, ultimately, we just want to be a positive influence in the community and do our part to keep it thriving. We started to sell baby chicks and egg-laying hens as an incentive to help others begin a small farm of their own and to hopefully learn for themselves along the way what it takes to put food on a table. Soon, we will have feeder pigs, baby chicks, and laying hens for sale. As we sell farm goods and animals, we hope to help other aspiring homestead farmers begin their own story of growing food for themselves and, in the process of it all, share the Kingdom of God with all of those we come into contact with.

That, after all, is the prime objective: to be fruitful and multiply.

The Big Lie and the Debt Monster

Of all of the things in life to overcome, one of the hardest is debt. We are programmed to believe that we need a certain level of "stuff" before we can be happy or even function in this world. I don't know. Maybe we do need some of the things that we have, but the older I get and the more I accumulate, the less I feel I need, oddly enough. I suppose, at some point, those two things will balance each other out, and I will no longer have any desire to seek anything new.

One thing is clear: when we die, we take nothing with us, so I think it's probably best for our families if we make sure we have very little as we near our time to depart this world. When my mom passed away, there was a house full of items to deal with and disperse.

Now, thankfully, even though we were a large family, there was no fighting over who got what. Mom and Dad were not wealthy people by any means, but there was a house full of "stuff." Thankfully, the house was very nearly paid off, and when it was sold, there was even a little to go around amongst 10 children. However, even if none of us got one thing or one dollar, we couldn't have been happier to have lived the life that Mom and Dad gave us.

Mom and Dad taught us how to be simple people and to enjoy the simple things in life, like a good cup of coffee in front of a warm fire or the pleasure of seeing a table full of food that was grown in our own garden. We didn't have a lot, but our house was full of love. So many people have been taught that the only way to live the good life is to acquire all the right "stuff," even if it means going deep into debt. In fact, the instant gratification machine tells us if you think it, you want it; if you want it, you need it; if you need it, you need it right now.

Life is short. Enjoy it while you can, and use plastic to do it. There is always the next new thing. You can have it now and pay for it while you enjoy it. Debt quickly becomes our master, and we work to pay the bills. The Bible tells us that the borrower is a slave to the lender. A slave! Slavery is illegal, right? Wrong! Slavery is everywhere today.

The banks own most of the population, and for those not deep in debt, many still use the banks for short-term loans and the like to keep acquiring more stuff—stuff that nobody wants as soon as you die. Even big estates are often not sought after by children because with them comes the burden of maintenance, upkeep, and management.

As Sue and I grow our businesses, we understand that if we don't set orders in place, one day, our children will be burdened with trying to figure out what to do with it all.

I have heard it said that the best plan is to grow your wealth until you have enough to get you to the grave with a penny left in your pocket. That's life to its fullest without leaving the burden behind.

Hebrews 11

I won't copy and paste the Scripture here. You can open up your Bible and read the chapter yourself, but this chapter is the key to the entire Christian faith. In fact, it is the chapter on faith. The writer not only provides us with the definition of faith, but also offers numerous life examples of key players from the Bible. It is written that without faith, it is impossible to please God. We must first believe that He is and that He is who He says He is and has done the things He has said in His Word. In order to believe what the Word says about God, we must believe that it is the inspired Word of God. If we don't accept this on faith, we can go no further with God. Having said this, it can be understood that Hebrews 11 becomes pivotal to the Christian Walk and to the overcoming of this world and Satan.

If we do not have faith, we cannot trust God to do what He says He will do. Much of the Christian Walk, if not all of it, requires us to trust God in the deepest, darkest moments of our lives and understand that it is at these precise moments that God reveals Himself to us. If we live such a careful life that we never come to a place where we must depend on Him, it is very difficult to say that we are living a life of faith. Faith is not, however, a display of recklessness. We cannot do things outside of God's will and expect Him to show up and save us from the pitfalls we enter by doing so. Faith is knowing that when we step out in a thing that God has sent us to do, even when we come to our end, He will not leave us; rather, He will carry us through. Jesus promised us that in this life, we will have suffering.

That is to say, we will experience hardship and trial. But he also said that He will never leave us nor forsake us. When all seems lost, He is there if we believe in Him and desire Him. It is essential that we get this concept down deep into our very bones so that when the hour comes that we are tempted the most, we will not even have another place to go to draw from. We can build great wealth, but it will not protect us from all of the diseases that can come and steal our lives away.

We can build our bodies to become so healthy and resistant to would-be invaders that no disease can enter, but it will not protect us when a semi-truck crosses into our lane and hits us head-on. We can become so insulated from the outside world that wars and famine cannot reach us, yet it will not protect us from an invasion of the sun's rays and drought that will kill all that we have. We are at the mercy of our Creator whether we admit it or not, and the only thing that can protect us from His wrath is the faith in Him that He will preserve those whom He loves and has loved Him. Our testimony is one of faith, faith in the one that has created all and redeemed all by His shed blood.

The Price of Success

When we look at all of the successful people in the Bible and life closely, we begin to see that there is certainly no one factor that can be pointed to obtain success. Faith in God, while probably the most powerful, will yield nothing if we do not act. Drive and ambition, while necessary, can push us into a place that is beyond our means.

Wisdom and understanding are critical to the recipe, but much like faith, if we do nothing in terms of motion or action all the wisdom there is will accomplish nothing. Action without a plan or vision of where one is headed can quickly take them into a place they never intended to go. Understanding the whole recipe is critical.

When Sue and I met up again at age 50, we had both received a college education, we had both raised families and been responsible for running a household and balancing a budget, we both had grown in our faith and understanding, and we had both applied all of this to corporate jobs in very big companies.

When we came together, God seemed to be moving us in a new direction, where all of the things we had learned in life to this point would be applied and experiences drawn on to build something new. Bringing our skill sets together seemed to be almost the most intuitive next step one could think of. We fit together so nicely, and the communication was instant.

Even before we were married, we had brought our skills together within 10 weeks. I was working on the flip houses, and Sue was shopping for farm equipment to take us to the next level. The farm deal was already at the closing table, and we were negotiating to purchase the church for the venue business. We can, together with the help of the Holy Spirit, without missing a stride while increasing the pace and adding multiple levels of complication to our now combined life. I am not sharing this to brag about it or to take glory in it, it is most important that God receives all the glory. This is also a critical component in the recipe for success.

So, now you may be asking yourself where in this is the price of success. Now that things are taking off the farm, the venue, and our marriage, we have become busier than we ever were as individuals. The pace is fast, and the stress can, at times, be high. However, when you learn to give God the glory, He will also take the burdens.

In other words, our success is not solely dependent on our efforts alone. God intervenes when He sees we need it, and he lets us suffer a little at times when He sees it will bring growth. Sue and I are now managing two businesses while she works a full-time job. The farm is very demanding in and of itself when you consider that we do everything from crop management to inventory management, marketing, animal care, and equipment maintenance, just to mention some of the business, not to mention all of the venue tasks of marketing, cleaning, maintenance of the building and the like. Needless to say, we are fully engaged all day, every day. While we do love what we do, at times, it can become overwhelming. God has equipped us for this over time and through lessons.

Hardships teach that dependence on Him is never to be underestimated. The overwhelming part caught up with me this past week when I ended up in the emergency room feeling like I may be having a heart attack. Earlier in the day, I had been working around the farm getting an area ready for some new chickens that we had gotten to expand our egg-producing capacity, and I am not sure if I did something then or if there was some other reason, but I began to have some pain in my chest area that felt something like heartburn. I wrote it off as such and kept on working, thinking it would pass.

When it didn't, I took some Pepto Bismol, but that seemed to have no effect. As the day wore on, the pain just got worse, and finally, that evening, while sitting down to watch a little bit of television with Sue, the pain got to a level that we decided I should get checked out. So, we went to the ER. They ran some tests, and everything came back fine. We were there until almost 1:30 in the morning. Later the next day, the pain had lessened, but still had not gone completely away. I concluded that I pulled some muscle in my chest and needed to rest it. There are all sorts of things that befall us, whether we work hard or not. But when we don't work hard toward success, we are certain to gain nothing for the hardships that are also certain to come our way.

Realizing the Person, You Want to Be

I think it is a pretty fair assumption to say that if you have been a Christian for a very long time, you have probably heard the term "God's calling for your life." That is God's purpose for you. I know I have spent many, many hours in prayer, seeking His will and purpose for me. God absolutely has a set purpose for each and every one of us, but He has designed us from the beginning with that in mind.

We have the ability to choose; in other words, we are given free will. It is God's desire that we have a sense of fulfilment and happiness in our lives, and this can be acquired while meeting His will or purpose for us. In fact, when we follow our God-given desires, it is only then that we will feel truly fulfilled. God has created everything to glorify Him, and when we are happy and fulfilled, we do just that. Have you ever given a gift to a child and they were not happy with it? How does that make you feel as the giver? When we exercise God's gifts in our lives, we give honor to Him and Glory.

Finding the thing that truly makes us happy in life can be more difficult than one may think. Satan has filled this world with traps. Things that, for a time, seem to bring happiness and fulfillment but quickly fade and become a prison. Drugs, sex, money, and careers, at times, can get out of control. While some things are absolutely forbidden, others only become sinful when they are taken to extremes and elevated above our love for God and others. Moderation is key, and priorities must be maintained to keep life in balance.

When we are young, there are so many new things to experience and try. My advice is to try as many things that are lawful as you can. Never be afraid of failure. Failure is necessary for learning. I have had many failures in life and have had a wide range of experiences. Learning to fly a plane, earning a Master's Degree, launching a new business and farm, raising children - the list goes on. But God has been faithful to catch me when I have fallen and has even promoted me at times when I have done well.

When we look into the lives of those in scripture, we see a plethora of failures and sins. We also see God acting on behalf of those same people to change not only their lives but many around them. When we don't try something, failure is certain. When we try, we may fail, or we may not, but when we try again and again, eventually, success comes. God is faithful to His word, and His word says that what you plant, you will reap in due time if you faint not. It is in the harvest that we find joy and happiness. In the parable of the talents, the only one that God was not happy with was the one who did nothing with the talents he was given. Use the talents you are given, build new talents by investing them, and when you see God, if you have done so to give glory to Him, you will be rewarded.

The Final End

When we read the book of Revelation, we see all kinds of great and terrible events that take place at the end of this age.

We see how God removes Satan and his followers from the face of the earth and how all of these events are brought forth to be a final judgment of mankind. In this book, the writer talks about a group of people who have come into heaven and are rewarded, and it says: "They overcame him by the blood of the Lamb and the word of their testimony." It could be thought that this is talking about the group that lives specifically at the end of days, but in fact, it could also be applied to all of those throughout all of history who have overcome Satan. It was always by the blood of the Lamb that this was made possible, and only by the blood of the Lamb.

The testimony is that they had faith in that blood and in God's ability and willingness to deliver them from the devil's wiles and the sins of this world.

As for any loose ends I may have left open in this book, such as the clarinet playing, I suppose you will have to look for the continuation in the next book.

www.ingramcontent.com/pod-product-compliance
Lightning Source LLC
Chambersburg PA
CBHW051209120626
46547CB00013B/1266